GUI DESIGN

SendPoints

GUI DESIGN
© SendPoints Publishing Co., Ltd.

EDITED & PUBLISHED BY SendPoints Publishing Co., Ltd.
PUBLISHER: Lin Gengli
PUBLISHING DIRECTOR: Lin Shijian
EDITORIAL DIRECTOR: Sundae Li
EXECUTIVE EDITOR: Felix Ma, Serena Siu, Catherine Wong, Yuanwen Zhong
ART DIRECTOR: He Wanling
EXECUTIVE ART EDITOR: Huang XiaoQiong, Lin Qiumei
PROOFREADING: Sundae Li, Heart Fensch

ADDRESS: Room 15A Block 9 Tsui Chuk Garden, Wong Tai Sin, Kowloon, Hong Kong
TEL: +852-35832323 / **FAX:** +852-35832448
EMAIL: info@sendpoints.cn

DISTRIBUTED BY Guangzhou SendPoints Book Co., Ltd.
SALES MANAGER: Zhang Juan (China), Sissi (International)
GUANGZHOU: +86-20-89095121
BEIJING: +86-10-84139071
SHANGHAI: +86-21-63523469
EMAIL: overseas01@sendpoints.cn
WEBSITE: www.sendpoints.cn

ISBN 978-988-13834-9-5

Designer

 Creative Director

 Art Director

 Photography

 Studio

 Client

 Country

 Website

Contents

Contents

Contents

GRAPHICAL USER INTERFACE DESIGN

To work with a given system, users should be able to control and assess the state of the system. And interactive products must be well thought out to support the way humans interact with the world and information.

The user interface (UI), the human-machine interaction in industrial design, is the space where interaction between humans and machines occurs. This interaction is to achieve effective operation, control of the machine on the user's side and feedback from the machine, which aids the operator in making operational decisions. With the ever-increasing use of personal computers and the relative decline of focus on heavy machinery, the term "user interface" mostly refers to types of graphical user interfaces (GUIs) that use windows, icons, and pop-up menus.

A GUI is a program interface that takes advantage of the computer's graphics capabilities to make the program easier to use. The first GUI was designed by Xerox Corporation at its Palo Alto Research Center in the 1970s. Xerox PARC developed the Alto personal computer in 1973. It had a bitmapped screen, and was the first computer to demonstrate the concept of GUI. But it was not until the 1980s and the emergence of the Apple Macintosh that GUI took on a more widespread usage. One reason for their slow acceptance was the fact that they require considerable CPU power and a high-quality monitor, which were prohibitively expensive until recently.

A powerful program with a poorly designed user interface has little value, and a well-designed GUI can usually free the user from learning complex command languages. On the other hand, many users find that they work more effectively with a command-driven interface, especially if they already know the command language. In addition to the visual components, a slick GUI also makes it easier to move data from one application to another. A true GUI includes standard formats for representing text and graphics. When formats are well-defined, different programs that run under a common GUI can share data. This makes it possible, for example, to copy a graph created by a spreadsheet program into a document created by a word processor.

PLANNING WITH GUI

When designing a program, the GUI for the user is one of the first things to consider, not the last. A primary goal of any digital project is to enable its users to have efficient and rewarding access to a collection. The project may be superbly created and organized, but if the GUI is not well designed, those advantages are unlikely to be of help.

A much better approach is to identify your users' needs at the beginning of the project, allowing those needs to dictate which collections of data you utilize and the functionality you require from your GUI. Instead of being an afterthought, the GUI should be planned out at the very beginning and should inform the way you create and catalogue your project.

Compromises will always need to be made. Standards and practices in GUI design have developed over time, so your current GUI should not entirely dictate your data capture and cataloguing practices. Ideally, your management of digital media objects (images, video and audio) and metadata should offer you some flexibility over the longer term.

Getting your users involved in the design of their GUI would be another goal when planning the GUI. Even if you've identified your users carefully, it is all too easy to make assumptions about what they need or expect from your collection. There is no substitute for asking them directly, not only at the beginning of your project but throughout its development.

Also be sure not to forget your cataloguers—they are also users and it is vital that you pay attention to their needs. Entering metadata is the very time consuming activity and over the course of a large project. When possible, make use of templates, default settings, drop down lists, bulk editing tools, automated metadata extraction tools or the ability to clone records. Simple things like enabling your cataloguers to tab through the fields rather than have to mouse-click, will save a lot of time.

BUILDING YOUR GUI

Having thoroughly researched your users' needs and explored a range of possible approaches, you need to assess what is going to be realistic given your current resources. A decision has to be made: will the GUI be built in-house, be off the shelf or will it be a combination of the two?

It is important to identify the limitations of GUIs (especially delivery and cataloguing interfaces) when you are sourcing an asset management system. It's also worth checking whether there is a proactive user group. Some asset management software companies have a good record of responding to requests from individual users or from user groups.

If you are building or commissioning your own delivery system, you will probably have more control over the look and functionality of your interface. However, this can prove an expensive and time-consuming process. Unless you already have the expertise within your team, you will need to find and hire someone with the relevant skills or train someone to do the work. The development is likely to take considerable time.

If you do take the route of developing your own system, you need to be very clear about your requirements, ensure that there is strong and effective project management in place and document everything fully. You must also make sure you have a plan for maintaining the delivery system once the project is finished.

ENSURING USABILITY

Usability draws on the field of Human Computer Interaction (HCI), which investigates the way people use computers. Usability is best thought of as a set of tools or techniques, rather than a set of rigid rules, although there are some relevant international standards.

Techniques for measuring the effectiveness, efficiency and satisfaction of a GUI can and should be used to test your own project at various stages throughout the design process, but there are some techniques that can be used to focus on the design itself. For example, you could investigate the End User Experience of your competitors to see what the users like or dislike about the design similar to the one you're developing. Or you could ask your users to organize and label your content and interface in the way that makes most sense to them. Of course, it would be also useful to ask users to evaluate models and mock-ups of your resource. That can be done by either using real or even dummy content.

ENSURING ACCESSIBILITY

Some people may face technological barriers to access, for a lack of resources or for their choice of technology. For example, your users may connect to your resource at a wide range of different speeds (dial-up modems to broadband or fast educational networks). If your resources require large downloads, it will not be very accessible for those with slow connections. Similarly, users may use a wide variety of devices to view your resource (from large screen monitors to digital televisions to mobile devices). If your collection is designed with the largest screens in mind, it may be inaccessible on the smallest.

Accessibility and usability can sometimes be harder to achieve if you have acquired an off-the-shelf digital asset management system to deliver your collection. Some systems offer little flexibility, forcing you to adopt color combinations, font sizes or layouts that hinder accessibility. Others offer good accessibility already or can be customized to achieve a suitable design. When purchasing a digital asset management system, you should make sure that accessibility and usability are highlighted on your checklist. It is well worth talking to system vendors about the issues. If the current version of their software has problems, it may be possible for them to incorporate improvements into future designs. It is in their interest to develop a product that meets user needs and satisfies accessibility.

Montagü

This visual identity project is for a Spanish-Mexican restaurant in Mexico City. The design reflects the use of rare spices and creative dishes through handmade type and unique illustrations that create harmony between ingredients, taste and design. Montagü started with an idea by Chef Roger Weber. The experiences he gleaned from his travels around the world gave him inspiration about how to shape the menu. It presents a unique character that collects flavors and ingredients from every corner of Asia, Africa, Europe and of course, Mexico. In part because of this project Weber has achieved his goal—his creations become a journey of flavors for Montagü's guests.

 Diego Leyva

 Diego Leyva

 Montagü - Gastro Winebar

 Mexico

 www.behance.net/nhomada

Noma Authentic

Noma Authentic is a side project from the world famous restaurant Noma. The concept is to create a culinary grandeur for people who want to learn more about utilizing the ingredients that can be found when hunting and fishing. One of the chefs from Noma will travel along to teach the participants about the area's resources and how to use them. The chef will also cook for the participants along the journey, so they will get a taste of Noma's great knowledge of food and cuisine.

When the participants arrive home from their journey, it will be possible for them to download an app which can teach them about resources that they can find in their own area. They can also see "resource marks" from participants on earlier trips so they can get pointers on how to be more self-sufficient. It will also be possible to make recipes for a dish that uses the specific resource that is marked in the users' area of the app.

 Jonas Emmertsen,
Henrik Ellersgaard

 Tim Cheneval, Brian Avery,
Corey Arnold, Mstudiofoto,
Lightbox, Marta Varela,
Nicolas Souche, Mikkel Adsbøl,
eybek.dk, Riccardo Guolo,
William A. Allard

 Denmark

 www.henrikellersgaard.com
 www.jonasemmertsen.com

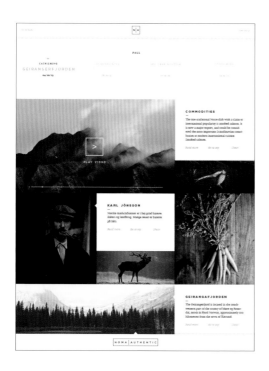

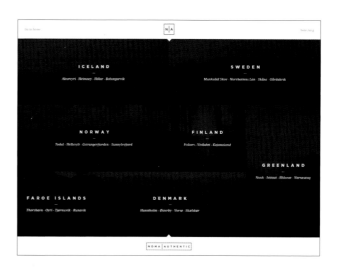

"We wanted the Noma Authentic project to be very minimalistic and Nordic without losing the exclusiveness of the Noma restaurant. We wanted to get the outdoor feel in the design, in which the images display. The fundamental style of the whole project is built on the image style and the typography."

Sivert Høyem–Website and Visual Identity

Sivert Høyem is one of Norway's most authentic and well-known musicians, a veteran of the Norwegian rock scene. He is best known as the vocalist of the band Madrugada. Soon after the breakup of Madrugada, Sivert embarked on a successful career as a solo artist, recording and performing internationally for over seven years. This project was initiated to take a new look at his image, by creating a bold and consistent brand that was flexible and could be used in combination with various image styles and artwork as well as on a variety of platforms (both digital and print). The logo system uses a clean typographic approach to allow for a modular system adapted for different surfaces and layouts. The website uses a minimalist, rigid grid system, which allows customization of color, type and image.

 Sindre Holm, Eric Amaral Rohter, Endre Berentzen, Robert Dalen

 Endre Berentzen

 Eric Amaral Rohter

 Anti Bergen

 Sivert Høyem

Norway

 www.siverthoyem.com, www.anti.as

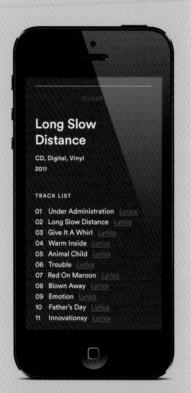
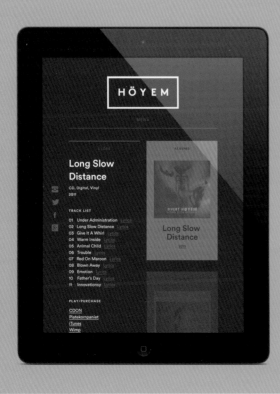
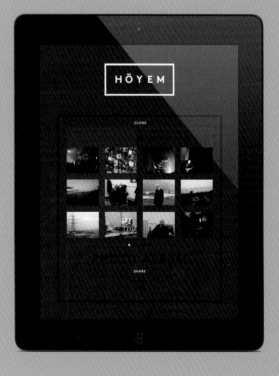

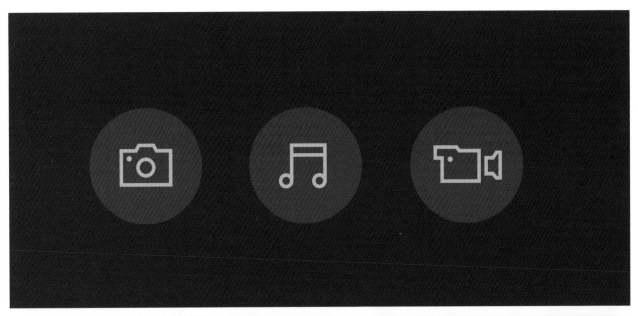

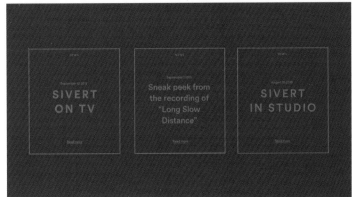

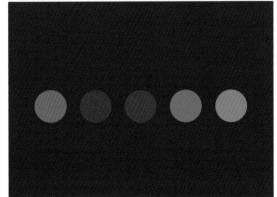

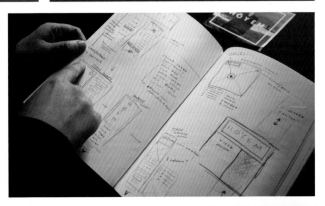

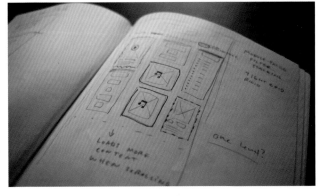

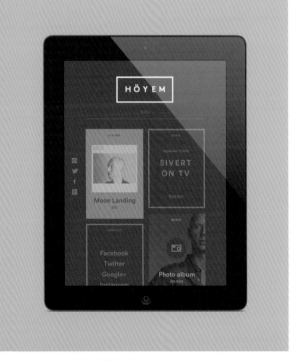

TRAVERSE

Train commuters constantly encounter unfavorable weather conditions, complicating their travel arrangements. To help deal with the problems, the designer created a social network mobile application called Traverse, which enables them to create and share weather-related poems while stuck in frustrating travel situations. They can upload their works through a live newsfeed and also comment on other people's creations by using this app, which should help to lessen the stress for the traveler.

 William Cundall

 William Cundall

 England

www.behance.net/WillisDesign

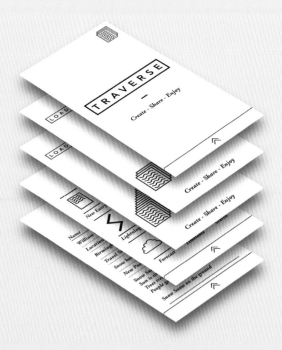

Authentic Weather

Authentic Weather was designed to be a realistic weather app. Instead of listing weather statistics only, the app presents actual photos of the weather situation. The camera mode allows users to share photos of different weather with friends.

 Tobias van Schneider

 Tobias van Schneider

 Tobias van Schneider

 Austria

 www.vanschneider.com

Authentic Weather

FOR YOUR IPHONE OR ANDROID

DAYTIME

It's
fucking
raining
now.

NIGHTTIME

It's
fucking
raining
now.

Probably the most honest & authentic weather app.

DOWNLOAD AT AUTHENTICWEATHER.COM

Fucking
love is in
the air.

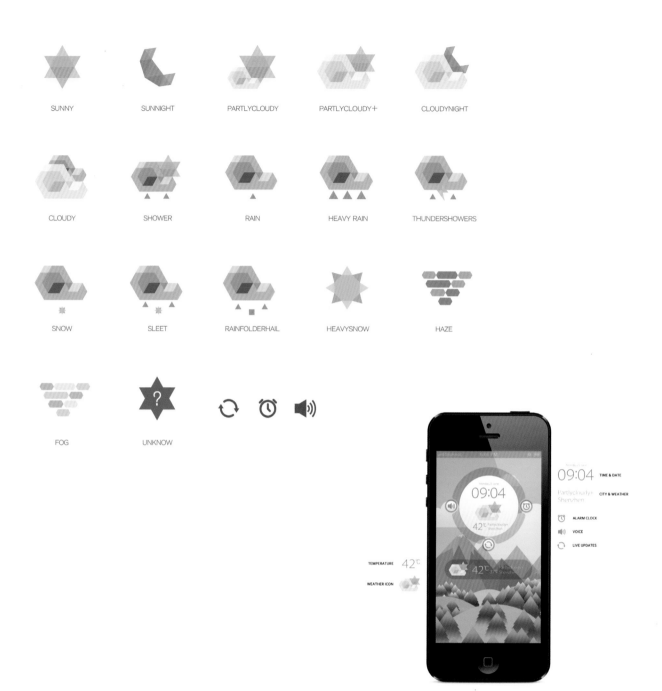

SUNNY   SUNNIGHT   PARTLYCLOUDY   PARTLYCLOUDY+   CLOUDYNIGHT

CLOUDY   SHOWER   RAIN   HEAVY RAIN   THUNDERSHOWERS

SNOW   SLEET   RAINFOLDERHAIL   HEAVYSNOW   HAZE

FOG   UNKNOW

Interesting Weather

This is a concise and active visual design for a weather forecast app. Without a fancy appearance or superfluous functions, it presents only useful information. The time and temperature appear on the home page with a white background while abstract but striking icons clearly reflect the current weather. The buttons for the refresh function, the alarm and the phonetic function are placed in a well-designed control area instead of in a crowded corner.

To vary the visual experience the designer created different wallpaper with dynamic representations for cloudy days, rainy days, snowy days, etc. These vivid wallpaper images change automatically based on the current weather.

Zhan Ying

China

www.zcool.com.cn/u/1437630

Weather CUBE

This is a minimalist design concept of weather forecasting for iPhone users. The highlight is the creation of intuitive interface without unnecessary elements and functions. The visual part of the application was used to depict the four seasons. It works on the presumption that the weather will change at different time of the day.

Kulikov Ilya

Russia

www.kulikov-design.ru

Dubai Agust 2012

☀ 🌡 **+32°**

749 mmHg   90%

◀ 5m/s

Tue 15	Wed 16	Thu 17	Fri 18
+32°	+38°	+36°	+37°

Berlin September 2012

☁ 🌡 **+13°**

749 mmHg   90%

◀ 2m/s

Tue 19	Wed 20	Thu 21	Fri 22
+14°	+16°	+14°	+13°

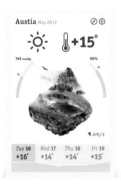

Austia May 2012

☀ 🌡 **+15°**

749 mmHg   90%

◀ 4m/s

Tue 16	Wed 17	Thu 18	Fri 19
+16°	+14°	+14°	+15°

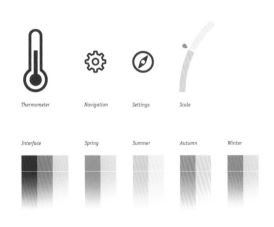

Moscow December 2012

🌨 🌡 **-12°**

749 mmHg   90%

◀ 2m/s

Tue 26	Wed 27	Thu 28	Fri 29
-12°	-15°	-10°	-12°

Thermometer	Navigation	Settings	Scale

Interface	Spring	Summer	Autumn	Winter

Sunny

Fair

Cloudly

Rainy

Thunderstorm

Sleet

Snow

Partly Cloudy

Partly Cloudy is a visualization-based weather app for iPhone. Its graphic design shows a weather forecast like an analog clock (12 or 24 hours) using color instead of lists of digits and icons. This allows users to see an entire day's weather situation at a glance. Partly Cloudy is an interesting example of the value of information visualization of everyday data on the iPhone platform.

 Timm Kekeritz

 Jana Kühl

 RAUREIF Berlin

 Germany

 http://partlycloudy-app.com

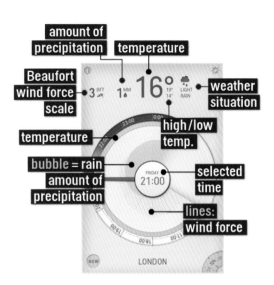

amount of precipitation

temperature

Beaufort wind force scale

weather situation

temperature

high/low temp.

bubble = rain

amount of precipitation

selected time

lines: wind force

LONDON

Helsinki

ABCDEFGHIJKLMNOPQRSTUVWXYZ
abcdefghijklmnopqrstuvwxyz
1234567890 !?@#&().,/ ° '

40 MM   5 BFT

RÍO GRANDE

LONDON

ROME

Derült égbolt	Erősen felhős	Közepesen felhős	Gyengén felhős	Borult
Szitálás	Gyenge eső	Eső	Ónos Eső	Záporeső
Havaseső	Hószállingózás	Havazás	Intenzív havazás	Hózápor
Száraz zivatar	Zivatar	Hózivatar	Jégeső	Párásság

Időkép

This app offers a long-range weather forecast service for Hungary. It involves a website and a mobile application. The designer updated the design of the mobile application for iOS7. He created a clear, flat style design so that users would not get confused searching and understanding the functions. The designer created a new icon set because he didn't want to use what can be found on the website for free.

 Attila Szabó

 Időkép

 Hungary

 www.behance.net/tremt

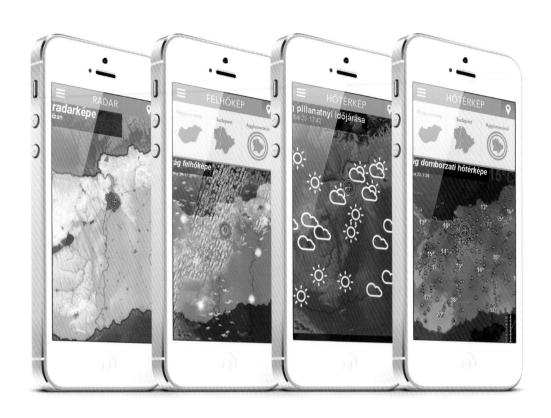

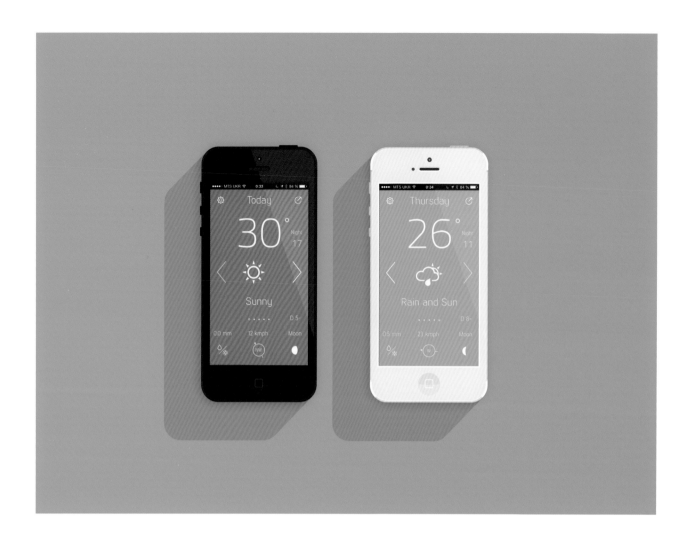

oWeather

With the social sharing function of this weather forecast app, users can share forecast via their social networks including Facebook, Twitter, Instagram, etc. The designers added stylish pictures and location into the posts along with users' comments to keep their friends updated with the latest forecasts. After the app was launched, the designers continued working on user interface improvement and bug fixes.

Artem Svitelskyi

KeepFive Design

Ukraine

 artsvit.com

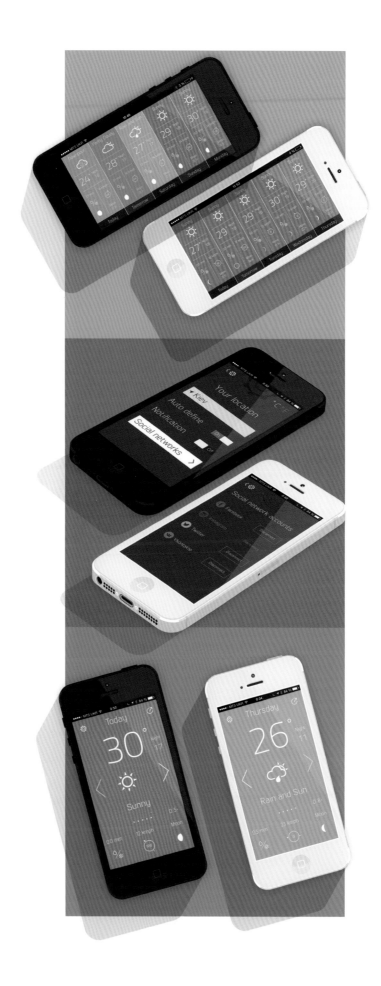

Main Screen

Settings

Day of the Week

Day Temperature

Precipitation

Wind Speed

Today

14°

Night
13

Partly Cloudy

D 10-

0.31 in   19 kmph   Moon

Social Share

Night Temperature

Weather States

Moon Days

Moon

↓ Slide down   ((📱)) or shake   ↻ to refresh

Main Colors

Rain

○ ○ ● ● ●

D 10-

0.31 in   19 kmph   Moon

SW

Calendars 5

Calendars 5 is a powerful and easy-to-use smart calendar for iPad and iPhone. Events and tasks are all managed in a single application, which is easily accessible. The goal was to create a perfect planner app that helps people to manage their time and life. Events and tasks are incorporated into the same place to work together. The clean and beautiful design should help people to focus on things that matter.

Dmitry Kovalenko

Dmitry Kovalenko

Readdle

Readdle

Ukraine

readdle.com

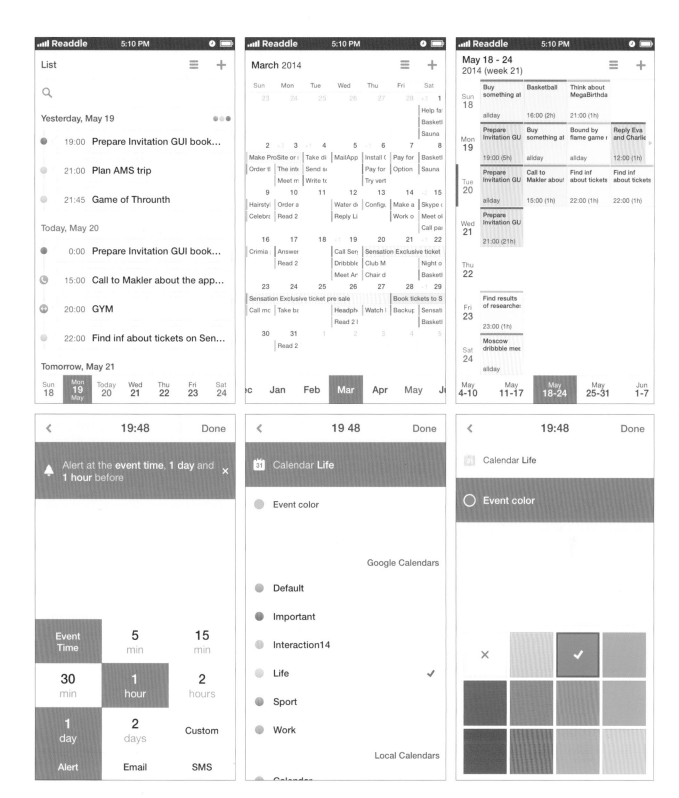

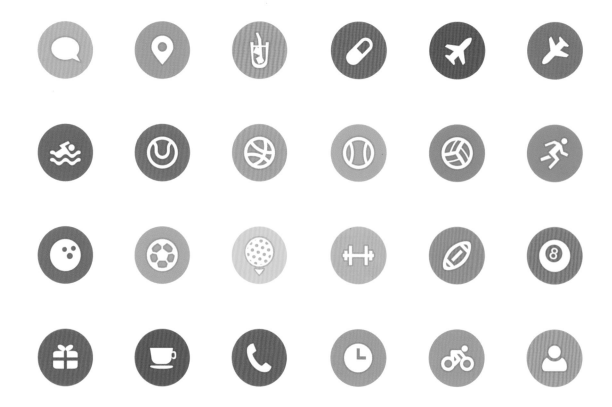

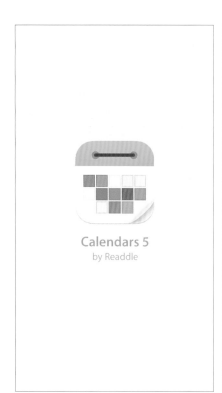

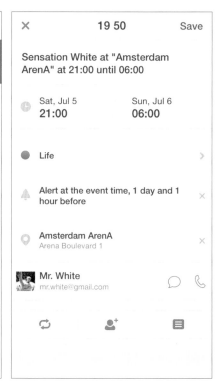

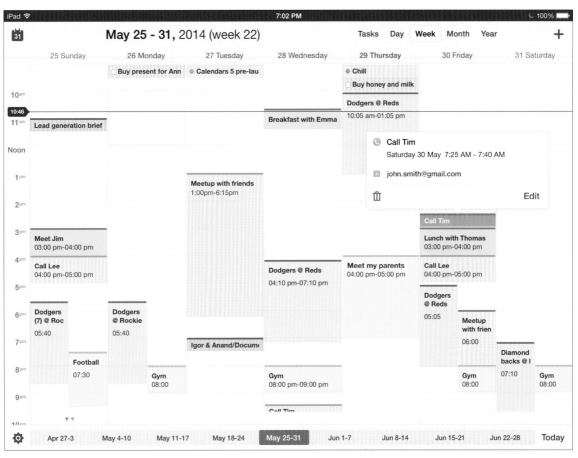

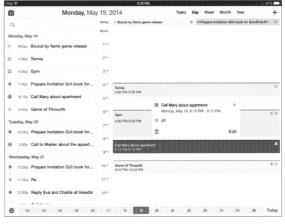

Peek Calendar

Peek is a quick and easy-to-use calendar for iPhone. It is easy to glance through and intuitive. The calendar presents the essentials in an easy-to-understand manner, without overwhelming people with data that they might not experience otherwise in an on-the-go life.

 Amid Moradganjeh

 Amid Moradganjeh

 Amid Moradganjeh

Estonia

 www.amidm.com

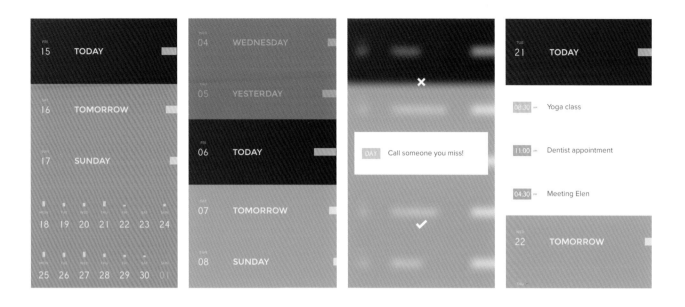

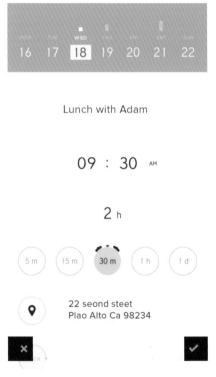

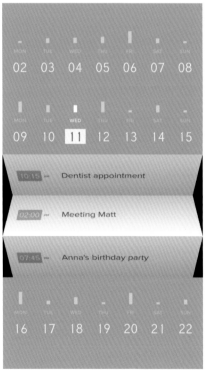

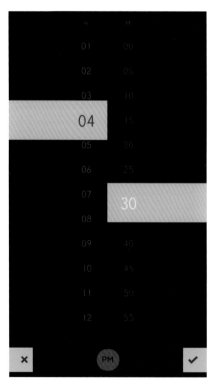

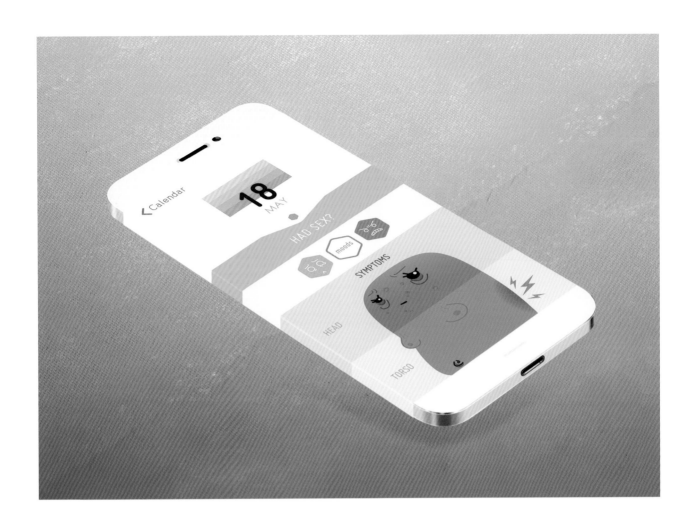

Period Tracker

Period Tracker is an iPhone app that tracks monthly menstrual cycles. Daily entries can be made based on everything from mood, symptoms and birth control reminders to sex life. The app analyzes women's past cycles and dynamically predicts future dates.

 Dianna Su

 Rebellion Media

 Canada

 dianna-su.squarespace.com

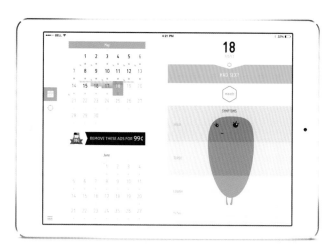

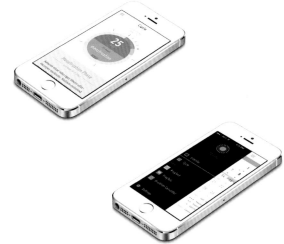

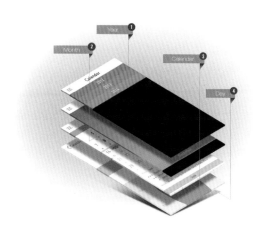

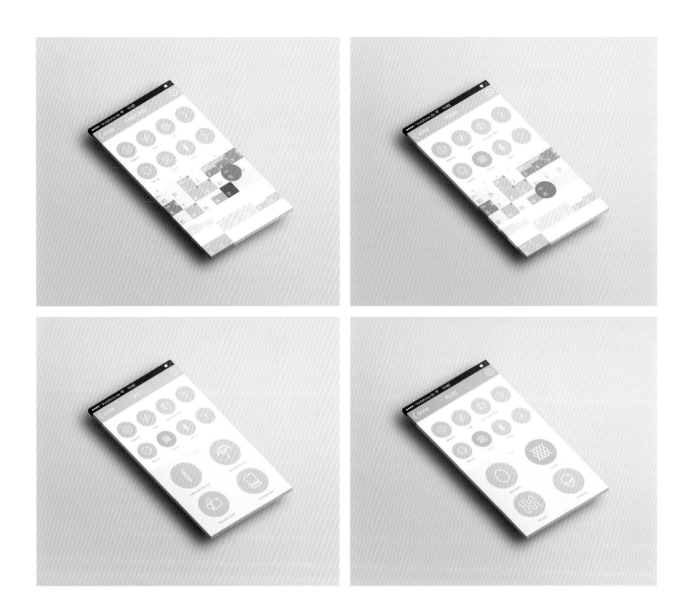

Clue

This design enables a fast, accurate and friendly process in tracking period. Users can make the best use of this app by entering data like cycle, pain, mood, sexual activity and so on.

 Luca Fontana

 Clue

 Italy

 https://www.behance.net/lucafontana

Retro Future Watches

Inspired by Dieter Rams, who helped to shape today's design industry, the creator of this project designed a lock app for iPhone. The clear use of colors along with an easy-to-use design helps this design stand out from other GUI designs.

 Luca Banchelli

 52minutes

 Germany

 www.lucabanchelli.com

Vital App

The Vital App offers an engaging experience, responding to its users "like a friend" through its aesthetically attractive, feminine design. It was developed for Vital, a German magazine that specializes in health and lifestyle. The app motivates its users to take the initiative in improving their own well-being. Daily updates with care tips for the body, mind and soul constantly change the appearance of the app. The user's achievements are visualized in beautiful animation as a means of encouragement. For example, the color and shape of an abstract flower are determined by the user's "VitaLevel". The Vital app was chosen by Apple as one of the "Best New Apps".

Katharina Stoltze, Alexander Meinhardt

Swipe GmbH

Jahreszeiten Verlag

Germany

www.swipe.de

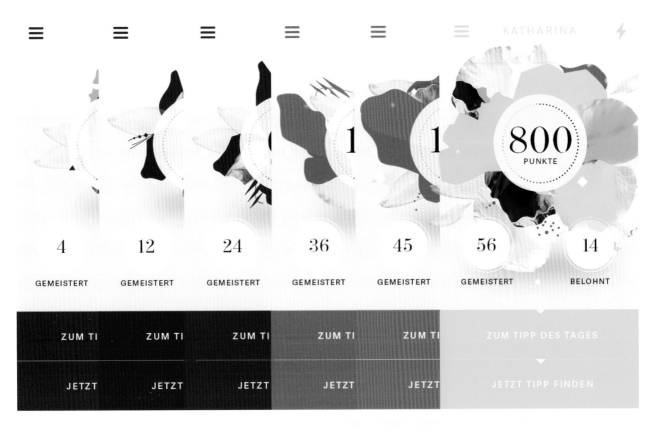

800 PUNKTE

4	12	24	36	45	56	14
GEMEISTERT	GEMEISTERT	GEMEISTERT	GEMEISTERT	GEMEISTERT	GEMEISTERT	BELOHNT

ZUM TI	ZUM TI	ZUM TI	ZUM TI	ZUM TI	ZUM TIPP DES TAGES
JETZT	JETZT	JETZT	JETZT	JETZT	JETZT TIPP FINDEN

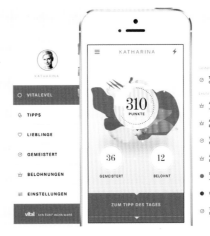

vita

FROM–Collect and Remember

FROM is a unique app designed to help people organize and catalog their gifts and cards all in one place. After receiving a present, people can use FROM to virtually store their special item, documenting it with pictures and details. Its organizing features can track everything from who, what, when, where and why to how people felt when they received the gift. Using FROM, people can share their response to a gift with friends via social media and send a beautiful thank-you card to the giver. Later, people can access all of the details about their gift using a variety of search features.

 Sooyeon Kim

 Sooyeon Kim

 USA

 www.callmesoo.com
www.from-app.com

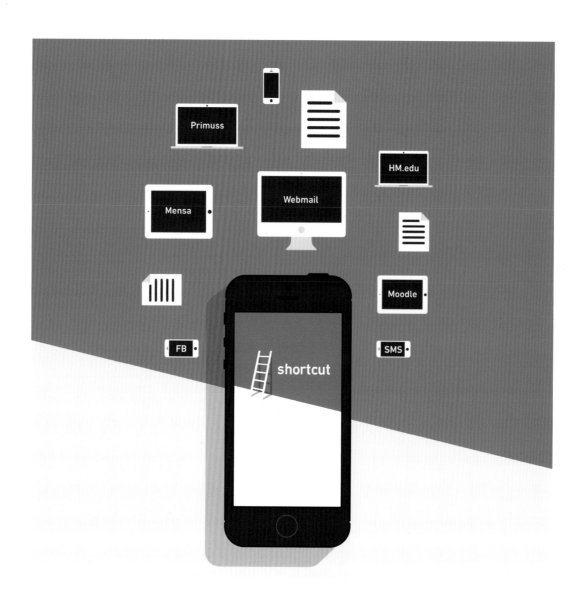

Shortcut University App

One of the most important skills students have to learn at university is the ability to organize things. But in order to do this they need the right information. Information is sometimes hard to reach, especially at the University of Applied Sciences in Munich.

To organize their studies, students have to collect information from multiple resources. Shortcut is a concept for an app that collects all the important information.

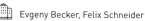Evgeny Becker, Felix Schneider

Evgeny Becker, Felix Schneider

Germany

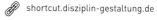shortcut.disziplin-gestaltung.de

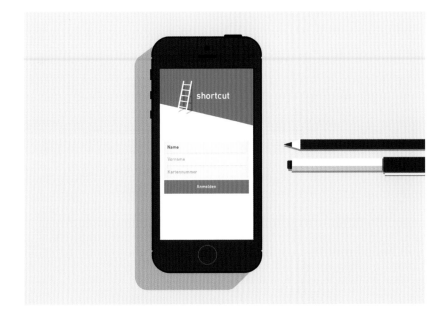

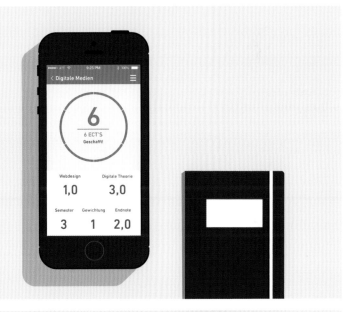

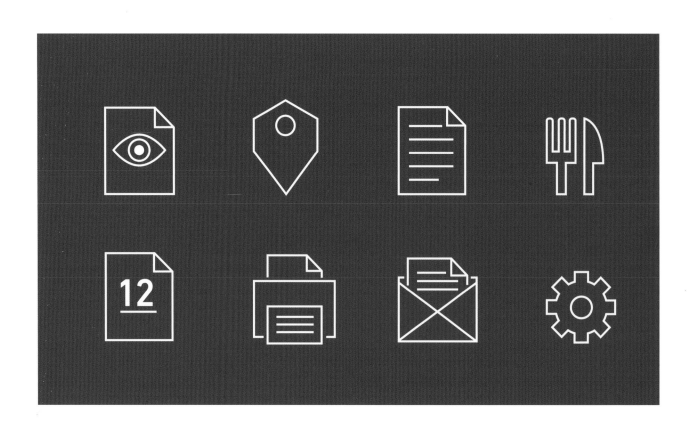

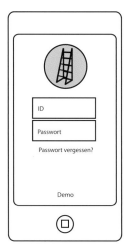

ID

Passwort

Passwort vergessen?

Demo

Kalender ≡

Woche	Monat

Datum

Uhrzeit	Fach	
Uhrzeit	Fach	
Uhrzeit	Fach	
Uhrzeit	Fach	

Menu ✕

◻	Kalender
◻	Verwaltung
◻	Fakultät XX
◻	Mensa
◻	Einstellungen

Mensa ≡

⟨ Datum ⟩

Gericht #1	€€€
Gericht #2	€€€
Gericht #3	€€€
Gericht #4	€€€
Beilagen#1	€€€
Beilagen#2	€€€

●○○○○

‹ Einstellungen ≡

Account	›
Fächer verwalten	›
Pushnachrichten	An/Aus
Info	›

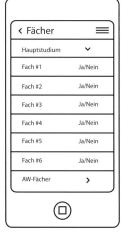

‹ Account ≡

ID	
Kennwort	
Eingelogt bleiben	Ja/Nein
Kennwort vergessen?	

‹ Fächer ≡

Hauptstudium	⌄
Fach #1	Ja/Nein
Fach #2	Ja/Nein
Fach #3	Ja/Nein
Fach #4	Ja/Nein
Fach #5	Ja/Nein
Fach #6	Ja/Nein
AW-Fächer	›

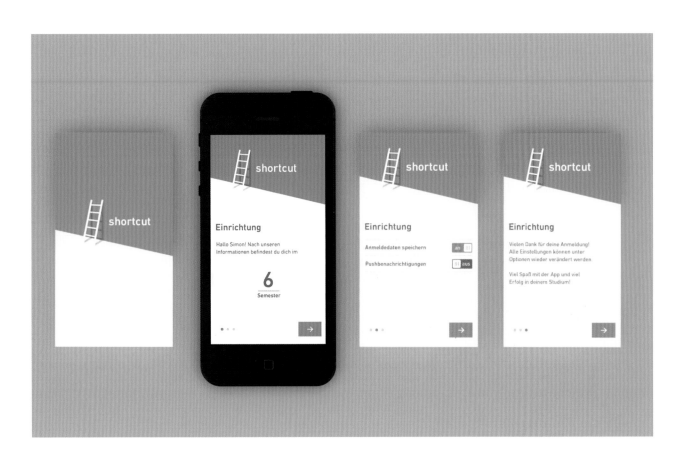

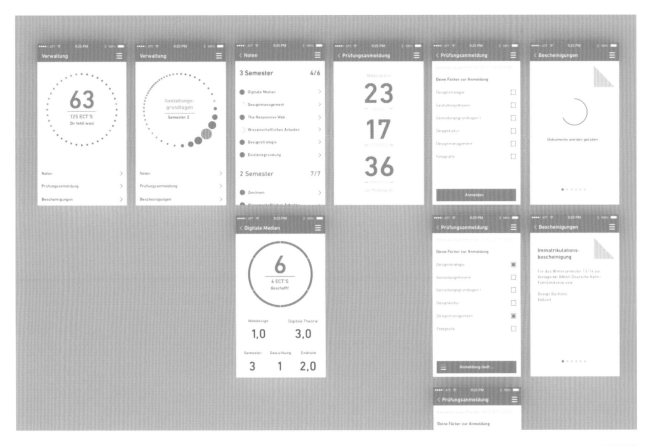

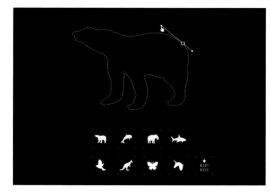

Anipedia App Concept

There are a lot of augmented reality app concepts on the internet. But many of them seem to focus on spying on people on the street. The idea behind the Anipedia app concept is to make augmented reality less scary and more educational for people. It is still technically unsupported, but the designer believes it very useful to be realized. Just point the crosshair on any animal to scan it, Anipedia will tell the user everything he/she needs to know about it. Then the user can save it to their own collection and compete with friends.

Filip Slováček
Czech Republic
slvczch.com

EQUUES

EQUUES is a mobile and web project to keep track of horses that are mainly for race, polo or other equine sports. Each horse has its own profile and important information input by people who interact with the animal. The user group consists of breeders, veterinarians, race and polo riders and the ones who participate in horses' daily care.

 Alejandra Bravo

 Germany

 be.net/AleBravo

App Menu Icons

App Icon & Launch Screen

Icons for App Users and Features

Tryptic Flyer

EQUUES

TECNOLOGIA DE LA
INFORMACIÓN EQUINA

Since this project is originated from Argentina, the logotype shows a "gaucho" figure who takes daily care of the horses. The colour palette, light blue and shades of brown, reflects the Argentine light blue sky, flag and the fur of typical horse breed.

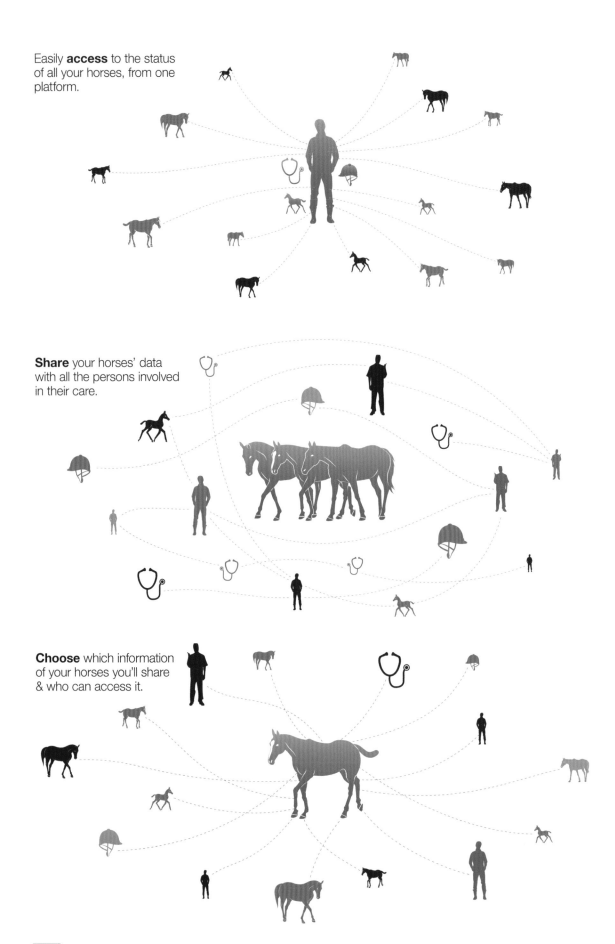

Easily **access** to the status of all your horses, from one platform.

Share your horses' data with all the persons involved in their care.

Choose which information of your horses you'll share & who can access it.

Administrá tu actividad ecuestre y guardá toda la información de **tus caballos.**

Veterinarios /

- Guardá todas tus **intervenciones**.
- **Organizá** todos los registros y datos en **historias clínicas individuales**.
- Asociá **radiografías, ecografías** y cualquier estudio adjunto con cada historia clínica.
- Administrá de forma ordenada tu **stock de medicamentos**.
- Planificá recordatorios para ejecutar tus planes **sanitarios**.
- Realizá **interconsultas** compartiendo toda la info del caso.
- Llevá un control prolijo de tus **gastos e ingresos**.
- **Facturá** de forma sencilla todas intervenciones e insumos gastados por cliente.
- Cruzá los datos, analizalos estadísticamente y tomá mejores decisiones.

Polistas / Jinetes / Cuidadores /

- **Organizá** los trabajos de tu veterinario, herrero y petisero.
- Llevá un control prolijo de tus **insumos y gastos**.
- **Administrá** de forma ordenada tu stock de insumos.
- Disponé de todos los diagnósticos de tu veterinario.
- Planificá tus **eventos** y **competencias**.
- Mostrá **fotos y videos** de tus caballos a terceros.
- Anotá todas las observaciones de tus caballos desde donde estés.
- Cruzá los datos, analizalos estadísticamente y tomá mejores decisiones.

Criadores /

- Organizá todos los datos de tu **manada**.
- Agrupalos por edad, por potrero y/o por cualquier criterio.
- Llevá registro de tus **nacimientos, servicios** y más.
- Planificá con recordatorios tus **vacunaciones** y **desparasitaciones**.
- Llevá un control prolijo de tus gastos e ingresos.
- **Administrá** de forma ordenada tu **stock de medicamentos**.
- Mostrá **fotos y videos** de tus caballos a terceros.
- Cruzá los datos, analizalos estadísticamente y tomá mejores decisiones.

Compartí

- **Explotá la riqueza de compartir la información** de distintos usuarios trabajando sobre los mismos caballos.
- **Cruzá datos** entre veterinarios, cuidador y criador te permitirá saber "los porqués" y tomar mejores decisiones.
- **Compartí toda la información** de tus caballos.
- Con diferentes grados de acceso, **elegí qué información compartir** sobre cada caballo.
- Mejorá la comunicación entre veterinarios, propietarios, jinetes y más.

Siempre DISPONIBLE.

Accede desde cualquier lugar y en cualquier momento a tus caballos desde internet sin tener que instalar nada.

Además, podés disponer de la aplicación **offline** en tu **smart phone y tablet** para carga y consulta de datos.

Así podrás guardar todas tus observaciones y registros en el momento, evitando olvidos y ganando tiempo.

Seguro y Confiable

Tus datos con la seguridad de un banco!

Toda tu información cuidada con los mejores estándares de seguridad.

La información viaja encriptada y se guardan back ups frecuentes.

Simple y Práctico

El sistema esta pensado y diseñado para que la carga y consulta sean ÁGILES y RÁPIDAS.

Con un par de clicks estas en la historia clínica de cualquiera de tus caballos y dejas todo anotado.

Flexible y Customizable

Vos definís qué te interesa medir o qué datos te anotaciones guardar.

Nosotros te brindamos la tecnología de la información necesaria para que la carga sea ágil y simple, para que su almacenamiento sea ordenado y seguro de manera que puedas posteriormente consultarla, analizarla y tomar mejores decisiones!

Paquetes de Servicios

PRUEBA	BÁSICO	PROFESIONAL
U$D **0** POR USUARIO POR MES	U$D **59** POR USUARIO POR MES	U$D **299** POR USUARIO POR MES
- Caballos ilimitados	- Caballos ilimitados	- Caballos ilimitados
- 3 etiquetas propias	- 3 etiquetas propias	- 3 etiquetas propias
- Historial de 6 meses	- Historial de 6 meses	- Historial de 6 meses
- Hasta 20 MB de adjuntos	- Hasta 20 MB de adjuntos	- Hasta 20 MB de adjuntos
- Registrá todos tus gastos	- Registrá todos tus gastos	- Registrá todos tus gastos
- Manejá tu agenda	- Manejá tu agenda	
Testear	Contratar	Contratar

* costo set up inicial: gratuito

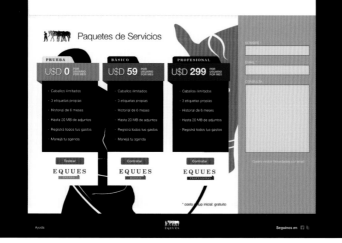

Plant Watcher

This application acts as a garden monitoring tool that can be a standalone device and users can interact with it through an additional mechanism other than the screen. This Garden Monitoring System, Plant Watcher, is able to help gardeners detect condition of their plants based on environmental and nutrient factors and provide them with necessary information to improve their plants' health. The clear and simple layout makes it user-friendly. A fresh natural flavor is created by the motifs of weather and leaves.

Kim-Anh (Ann) Le

United States

https://www.behance.net/kimanhle

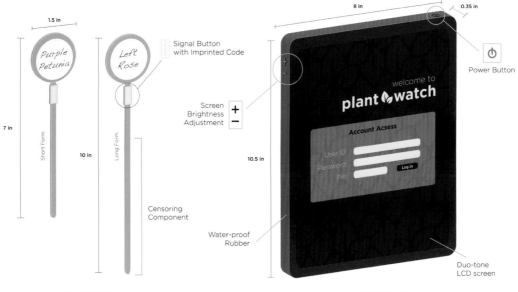

DETECTORS

SMART PAD

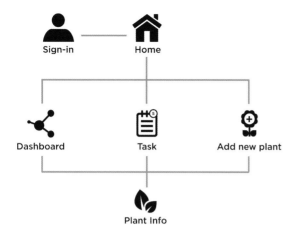

Sign-in — Home

Dashboard | Task | Add new plant

Plant Info

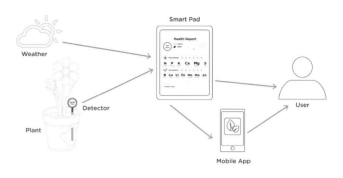

Weather

Smart Pad

Health Report

Plant

Detector

User

Mobile App

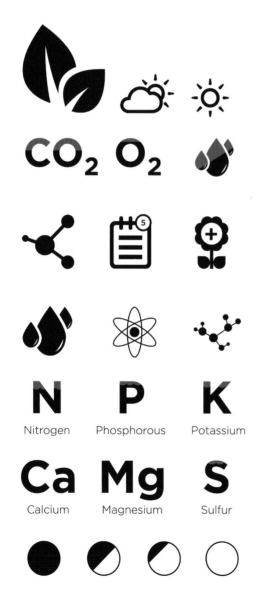

CO_2 O_2

N
Nitrogen

P
Phosphorous

K
Potassium

Ca
Calcium

Mg
Magnesium

S
Sulfur

plant watch
8:53 AM
CURRENT CONDITION

9 AM 10 AM 11 AM 12 PM 1 PM

Temperature
42°F | 6°C

Sun Exposure

Air Quality
CO_2 O_2

Humidity
51%

Dashboard | Tasks | Add new

welcome to
plant watch

Account Acsess

User ID:
Password:
Pin: Log in

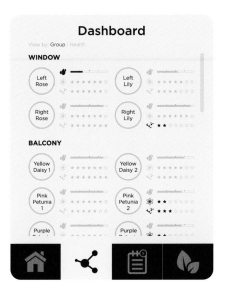

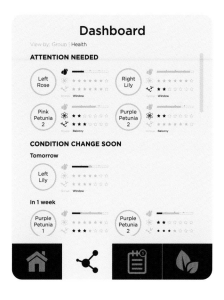

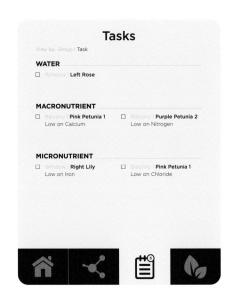

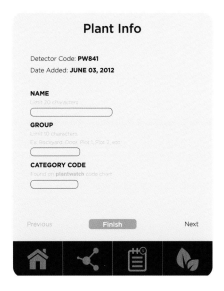

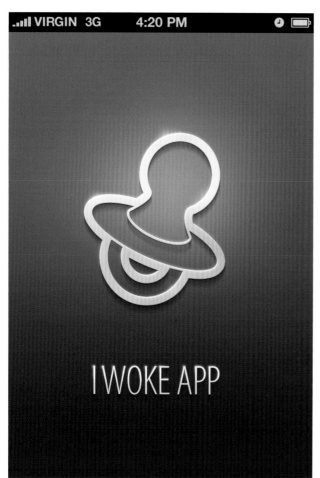

I Woke App

I Woke app is a cute little application designed for couples with a newborn to make life just a little bit more interesting. The idea was to create a "baby raising contest". The designer used a cool color scheme and simple elements to design the interface and make it seem distinctive. A set of cute icons for the interface created a delightful appearance of the application.

Roy Rachamim

Mor Shani & Ilay Avni

Mor Shani

Ilay Avni

Israel

www.hamutzim.co.il

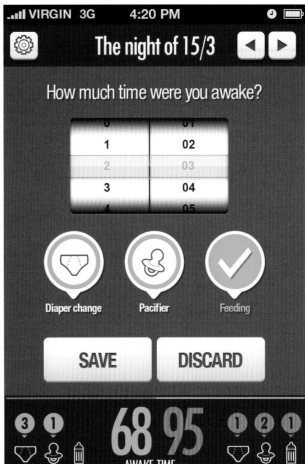

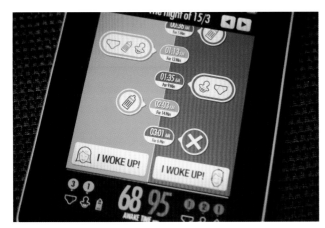

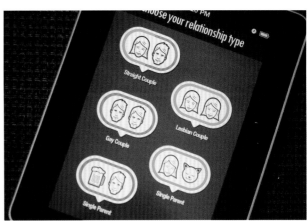

Appatente Nautica

This app helps the user in acquiring a boating license. Taking user experience into consideration, practical examples like the video of the most common nautical maneuvers, along with sea map sections and Coast Guard news updates are featured in the app. The user can also invite friends to join his boat trips.

 Francesco Galvan

 Luca Vidale

 Marco Volpe

 Crispy Bacon srl

 Italy

www.crispybacon.it

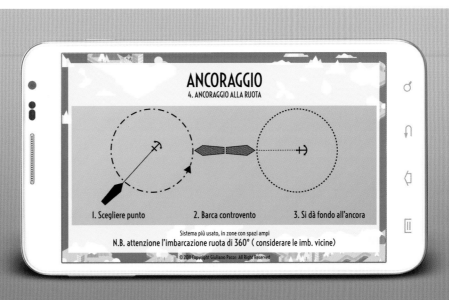

ANCORAGGIO
4. ANCORAGGIO ALLA RUOTA

1. Scegliere punto   2. Barca controvento   3. Si dà fondo all'ancora

Sistema più usato, in zone con spazi ampi
N.B. attenzione l'imbarcazione ruota di 360° (considerare le imb. vicine)

ANCORAGGIO
3. TIPI DI ANCORA

CQR (o ad aratro)
Tra fuso e marra c'è uno snodo e pertanto deve arare per qualche metro per assumere la posizione corretta e fare una buona presa. E' buona in tutte le condizioni.

GRAPPINO
Ottima su tutti i fondali, ma è sicuramente la più ingombrante e pericolosa da tenere in coperta.

DANFORTH
Leggera, ottima sulla sabbia. Poco efficace sugli scogli o sulle alghe.

BRUCE
Ancora fissa, ottima su tutti i fondali. Ha una patta centrale e due laterali sagomate.

Indice   Vai a...   cartografia

Download Aggiornamenti   Lezioni Pratiche   news guardia costiera

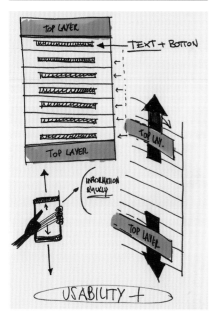

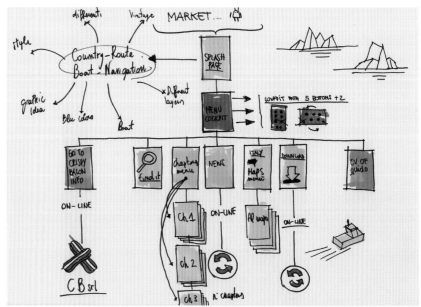

APPATENTE NAUTICA

diventa il comandante
tuo smartphone e naviga tra i contenuti
della nostra app

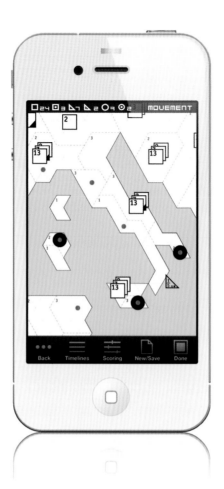

Timelines

Timelines is a video game for the iOS platform. The project focuses on the study of interfaces for mobile devices with multi-touch screen. The reduced display size and the haptic nature of the devices lead to the necessity to rethink everything we know about accessibility and usability to achieve an optimal user experience. The video game is a turn based strategy game that draws inspiration from "old school" board games like "Advanced Civilizations". The goal is to create an application that can be used comfortably with a single hand, and a gameplay is structured for short multiplayer turns so that the players can enjoy it even on short trips.

Rubén Santiago Vicario

Spain

https://www.behance.net/soyrubensantiago

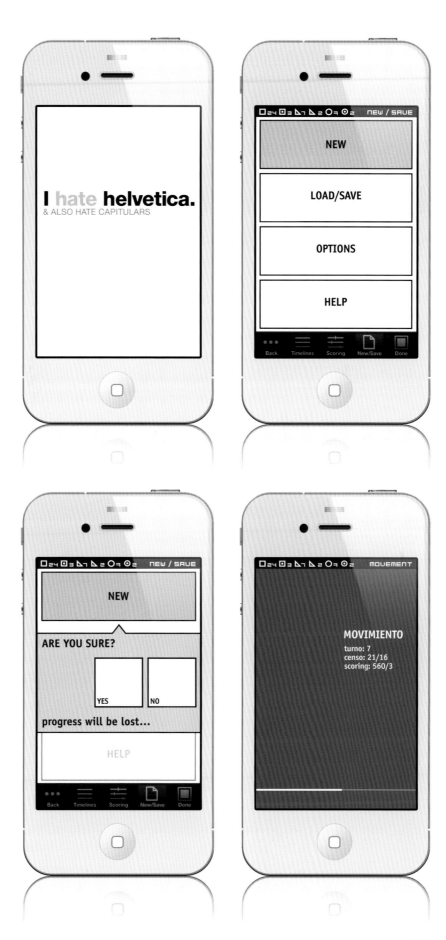

[04] CARGAR/SALVAR PARTIDA
Tap el load/save

[05] HELP
Despliega opciones para juego nuevo

[06] HELP EXPANDIDO

[4] TIMELINES

[5] TIMELINES (DETALLE)

[6] SCORING

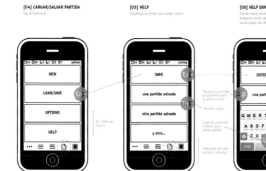

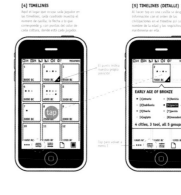

[13] ADVANTAGES

[14] ADVANTAGES (DETALLES)

[15] VOLVER AL MAPA

[08] OPCIONES

[09] HELP

[10] HELP EXPANDIDO

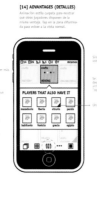

[13] DISASTRES

[14] HELP

[01] ELEGIR NACIÓN

[02] DESPLIEGUE INICIAL

[01] MOVIMIENTO

[02] INTERACCIÓN CON EL MAPA

[03] HELP

[03] HELP

[05] HELP

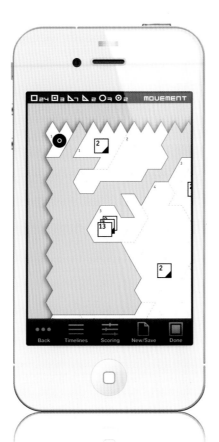

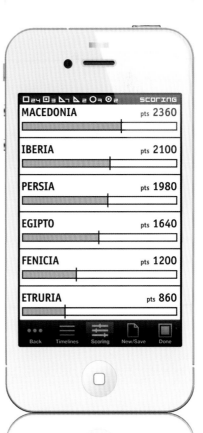

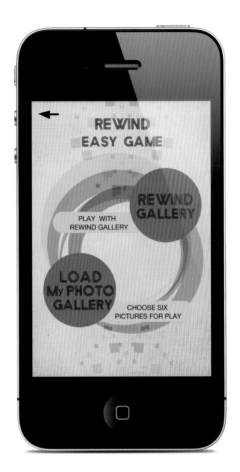

Rewind/ Remind

This project is a picture memory game for iPhone. The designer wanted to create an interesting game that exercises the user's memory. Users could either play using the "Rewind Gallery" or choose pictures from their own photo albums. To make the app more visually attractive, the designer mainly used polychrome spots and dots to decorate the interface, and then constructed a fun atmosphere that could match a happy game.

 Esther Pérez

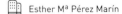 Esther Mª Pérez Marín

 Murcia, Spain

 http://cargocollective.com/chaika

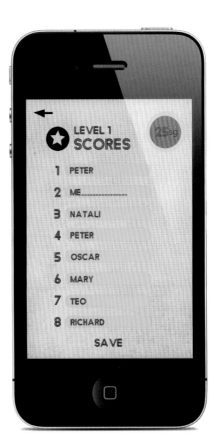

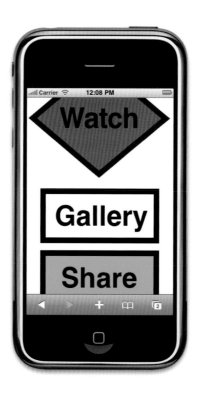

MoMA PS1 Pole Dance

SO-IL's Pole Dance is a summer-long outdoor social and spatial project for MoMA/ PS1 Young Architects Program. It was conceived to merge physical and auditory experiences through an integrated and interactive experience. The pavilion was comprised of flexible graphite poles covered with netting that contained a landscape of hammocks, a water misting system, pools and plants. Eight accelerometers were installed on the poles. By moving and shaking the poles, visitors could activate sounds that were played within the space. 2x4 designed an identity system and website for the project, as well as an iPhone application that allowed visitors to collaboratively control the sounds generated in real time, create live diagrams that tracked the moving poles, and effortlessly share their work online.

Yoonjai Choi, David Yun, Michael Squashic, Kees Bakker, Jonathan Lee, Kostadin Krajcev

Michael Rock

Jonathan Lee and Yoonjai Choi

2x4

SO-IL

USA

http://2x4.org/

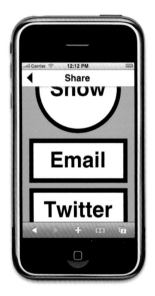

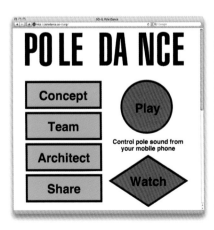

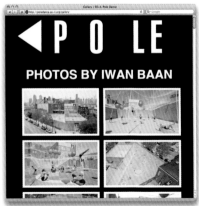

24h GUIDE   **24h** GUIDE   **24h** GUIDE

24 Guide App

Analysis of statistics by the Polish Ministry of Tourism showed that trends in tourism in the country are strengthening. This inspired the designers to create a project targeted at people who take short business or tourist trips. A notable feature of the application is that it can be updated with the instant information of the traveler's location whenever necessary throughout the day. With the technique of augmented reality, a quantity of instant information about the users' surroundings could be accessed by a simple scan of the space. All the functions help meet travelers' needs in the city.

 Piotr Szencel

 Jacek Mrowczyk

 Inklu Design Lab

 Poland

 http://www.inklu.pl

24h GUIDE   **24h** GUIDE

MAIN MENU BUTTONS

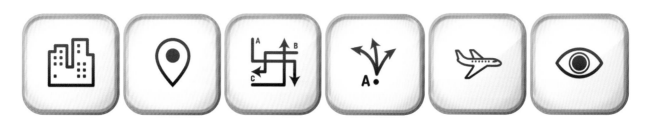

ICONS

NEWS	RESTAURANT	HOTEL	SHOPPING
TRAIN	TRAM	BUS	TAXI
AIRPORT	DEPARTURES	ARRIVALS	HISTORY

ADDITIONAL ELEMENTS

500m

1500m

MENU BAR

TAXI

Wybierz sieć >

Zamów
Znajdujesz się na ulicy: **Wojewódzka**

MAPA | TRANSPORT MIEJSKI | T. KRAJOWY

Filtracja >

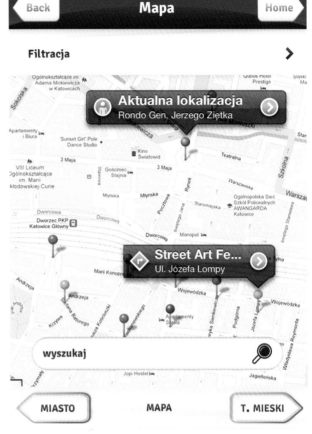

Aktualna lokalizacja
Rondo Gen. Jerzego Ziętka

Street Art Fe...
Ul. Józefa Lompy

wyszukaj 🔍

MIASTO | MAPA | T. MIESKI

---

znajdź nr lotu 🔍

14.45	London	
VR 602	TACV	DEPARTED: **15:42**
15:15	Zurich	
LX 206	SWISS IN...	DEPARTED: **15:37**
15:45	Porto	
TP 197	TAP POR...	CLOSED
16:00	Faro	
TP 193	TAP POR...	GATE OPEN

T.KRAJOWY | LOTNISKO | WIZJA

---

znajdź nr lotu 🔍

| London | | 14.45 |
| VR 602 | Z KTW PYRZOWICE | DEP: **15:42** |

| TERMINAL | CHECH IN | BRAMKA |
| **T1** | **41 – 44** | **17** |

✈ SWISS International

📞 + 351 707 205 700

🌐 Odwiedź stronę www

T.KRAJOWY | LOTNISKO | WIZJA

The Green Belt Guide

The Green Belt Guide App was inspired by modern tourism and serves as a tool for tourists to follow the old trail of the Iron Curtain in Europe, most of which has become a new Green Belt. The design style was intended to remain simple and minimalistic while stay focused on the use of icons.

 Alina Kotova

 Molly Radecki

 Czech Republic

 https://www.behance.net/AlinaK

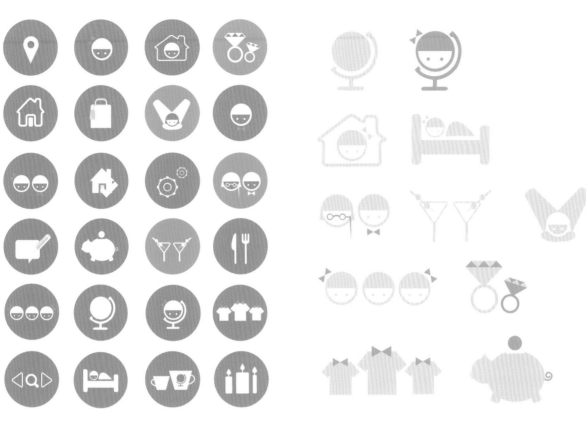

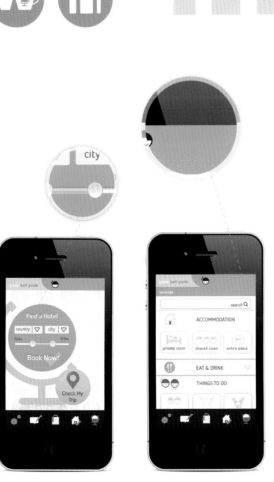

ANA Airport App

This project consisted of functional design, creative process and technological implementation of the app for the Airport Authority of Portugal (ANA). The app features real-time flight information and useful information on leisure time and shopping to passengers. Even when not logged into the app, passengers could keep being updated of the status of the flight through push notifications.

The design ensures a simple and easy-to-use interface and also recommends some popular destinations. The navigation concept is based on the cardinal points: north, south, east and west, referencing air navigation.

Carla Marta Moreira,Luís Trindade,Tiago Lopes,Daniel Pereira,Diogo Cera,Paulo Borges

João Oliveira Simões

Innovagency

ANA Aeroportos de Portugal

Portugal

www.innovagency.com

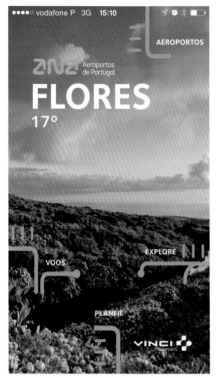

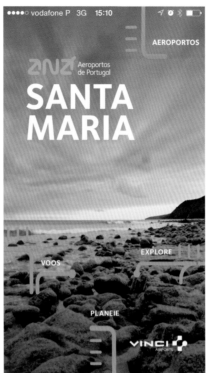

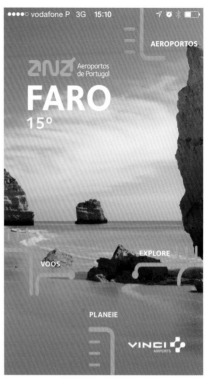

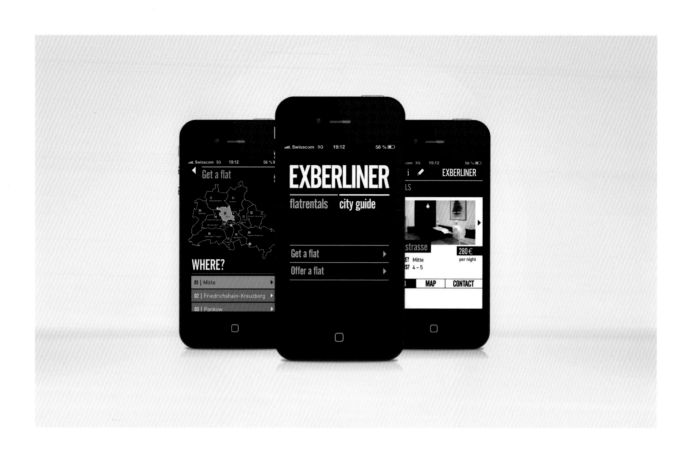

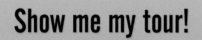

Exberliner Tourist App

Inspired by the flat interface design in 2013, the designer created an optimized app for the Berlin Website "Exberliner Flat Rentals".

Raïssa Lara Fasel

Etvoila Design

HFK IAD Höhere Fachschule für Kommu-nikationsdesign, Interaction Design

Switzerland

www.behance.net/etvoiladesign

Public Transportation in Izmir

"İTTH" stands for "İzmir Toplu Taşıma Haritası" (Izmir Public Transportation Map). It's an application created to help citizens and tourists in Izmir when using public transportation. It shows the shortest route to the place people want to go in Izmir. It also estimates when the vehicle (bus, metro, ferry) will arrive at the location.

Dogacan Ege Altunsu

Citizens of Izmir

Turkey

www.dogacan.com

Vapur

Metro

Otobüs

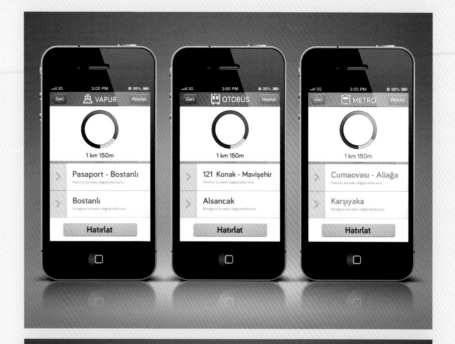

HopCab App

Hopcab is a taxi booking app for Malaysia, currently available in Kuala Lumpur and Penang. Users can view surrounding taxis and estimate fares in advance. After that, they can save the routes and view the past trips.

Admir (Adi) Dizdarevic

Hipinspire agency for HopCab

Bosnia and Herzegovina

www.dyya.tv

Cycling App Concept

The project started with the question: "how can we make something so simple that it can show all the necessary information in just one or two actions or screens?" It's all about creating a product that doesn't need instructions or navigation map.

The designer wanted this app to be different from many apps for cyclists on the market which are based on the same template. His idea was to create something that features the simplicity of flat design and combine with the classic feel of an organic element. The app was based on a play with the opacity of the elements, and combinations of black and white shapes.

 Alexandru Stoica

 Romania

 https://www.behance.net/alexandrustoica

About

Around Me

Tag The Line

Guide

Profile

Shopping

Eat & Drink

Green Spots

What's Happening

Take Action

Let's Get Schooled

The Urban Green Line

The Urban Green Line (UGL) connects people, green spaces and organizations with each other. At the same time it encourages walking, co-creation and urban gardening along the way. Looking to expand from their offline grassroots community work, UGL approached Transfer Studio on helping them to harness the spirit of a wider online community.

After a long and fruitful period of consultation, the designers assisted UGL in disseminating their vision into clear concepts with tangible outcomes, and developed their main digital platforms. A user-friendly iPhone app and website with accessible navigation were created which allowed users to continue to cultivate their mission of urban sustainability.

Falko Grentrup, Valeria Hedman

Transfer Studio

The Urban Green Line

Sweden

http://transferstudio.co.uk/

Directory

Selected Category

Around Me/List

Around Me/Map

Green Spot

Image Preview

Comment

Urban Cycle

Urban Cycle is a smart phone application for international use. The primary goal is to provide visible routes to cyclists in their cities. After getting on a bike, the user can press the big green "UC" button to turn on the "Tracking" function and it will start to track the journey. After the trip, the user can check the statistics and all the routes that have been tracked, and also the other biker's routes in the same city or in any other locations where Urban Cycle has been used. As an extra service, the "Poster" item allows users to create the final routes as a graphic image.

 Gergely Hangyás

 Hungary

 https://www.behance.net/aeneis

BIKE BADGES OF THE WORLD

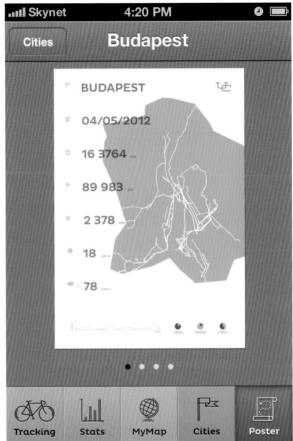

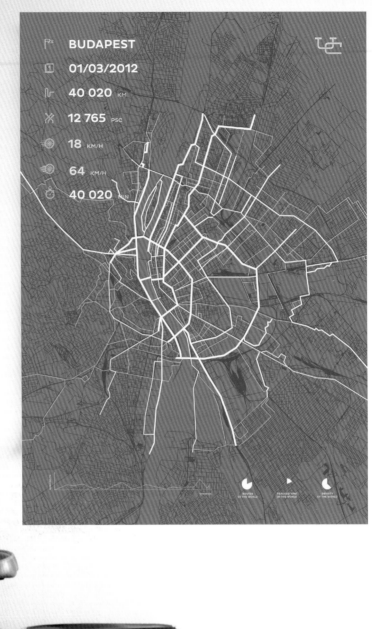

BUDAPEST

01/03/2012

40 020 KM

12 765 PSC

18 KM/H

64 KM/H

40 020 MIN

CalcFLO

"The same result, but different experiences." is the theme behind CalcFLO—an iOS calculator app available for iPhone and iPad. The main purpose was to give users fresh-looking app features which were not offered by the iOS calculator. CalcFLO is equipped with memory, allowing users to easily save the results and use them in the future. Another important feature is that CalcFLO is designed on the basis of a standard calculator layout so that the app does not require learning new habits. To cater to users' tastes, the app offers colorful themes.

Karol Ortyl

Patryk Sobczak

SkyFlo Apps

Poland

www.karolortyl.pl

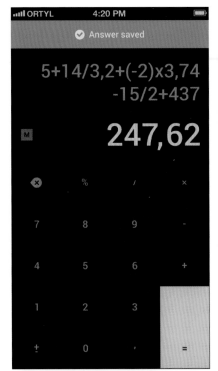

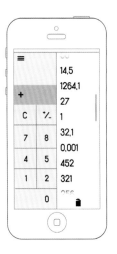

less than yesterday

same as yesterday

more than yesterday

Counter for AdSense

The core aim of the app was to give users a way to keep track of their AdSense activity intuitively and painlessly. How to cram lots of data onto the screen of a smart phone became a question to the designers. They decided on a visual approach and came up with an app that lets a person see AdSense results visually through the movement of numbers and color changes in the display. That concept drove the app's entire development, from GUI design right down to its architecture.

 Ivan Klymenko

 Stanfy

 New York Entrepreneur

 USA

http://stanfy.com/

Login to Google AdSence

Login

Settings

adsenceapp@gmail.com

●●●●●●●●●●●

Logout

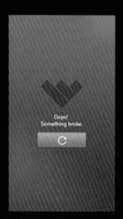

Oops!
Something broke.

C

7589 34

08 October, Monday

• 3547,88   00:00
  3435,69   23:00
• 3368,14   22:00
  2785,76   21:00
  2685,75   20:00
  2333,32   19:00
  2207,22   18:00
  1998,61   17:00
  1823,56   16:00

3547 88

09 October, Tuesday

• 3547,88   00:00
• 3435,69   23:00
  3368,14   22:00
  2785,76   21:00
• 2685,76   20:00
• 2545,71   19:00
  2445,23   18:00
  2327,45   17:00
  2203,04   16:00

3878 56

Today, 23 October

3878 56

Today, 23 October

354788
Yesterday, 22 October

12354673,4
This month, 01-23 October

9876543,25
Previous month, 01-30 September

3458 56

Today, 23 October

3841 68

Today, 23 October

3878 56

Today, 23 October

• 3547,88   00:00
  3435,69   23:00
• 3368,14   22:00
  2785,76   21:00
  2685,75   20:00
  2333,32   19:00
  2207,22   18:00
  1998,61   17:00
  1823,56   16:00

Home

History

Statistic

Today

Kount.ly

How many books have you read? How many times have you been to the movie theatre? How many trips have you made? How many restaurants have you been to this year? With Kount.ly you are able to count everything. Also, you can add a comment to each item you make, follow the progression on a chart and share it with your favorite social networks.

 Olivier Pineda

 Seempl Studio

 France

 http://seem.pl

Dashboad
+ All your Kounters at a glance

List view
+ You can : count, archive and delete

Create
+ Add a new cool kounter

Single view
+ Find your Kounter history
as well as your comments

Kount•ly

Kount•ly

205
Restaurant

5	Cinema
168	Coffee
3029	Books
23	Restaurant

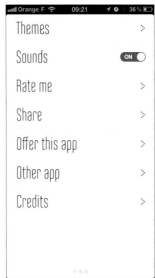

Themes	>
Sounds	ON
Rate me	>
Share	>
Offer this app	>
Other app	>
Credits	>

Restaur_

5	Cinema
168	Coffee
3029	Books

168
Coffee

168	Saturday, September 5 2012 at 4:16 p.m.
167	Monday, Septembre 1 2012 at 8:12 a.m.
166	Sunday, August 31 2012 at 9:26 a.m.
165	Friday, May 22 2012 at 8:47 a.m.
164	Monday, January 24 2012 at 9:34 a.m.
163	Tuesday, January 12 2012 at 12:41 a.m.

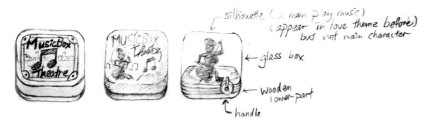

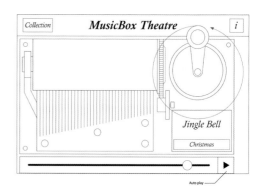

Musicbox Theatre

Like a traditional music box, Musicbox Theatre app allows users to play songs manually at a speed controlled by a simulated handle, recreating various famous songs. Musicbox Theatre is not only a music player, but also a story teller. The designers created a light box inspired by traditional Chinese "shadow plays" ("皮影戏"), matching different music with different theme characters. Users can control the tempo of the music and the silhouettes. The user experience involves not only listening to the music, but also enjoying fantastic journeys with different themes.

Terence Chung

Chin Yiu Chau, Patrick To, Terence Chung

Hong Kong, China

www.apperdeen.com;

http://www.behance.net/gallery/ MusicBox-Theatre/10435419

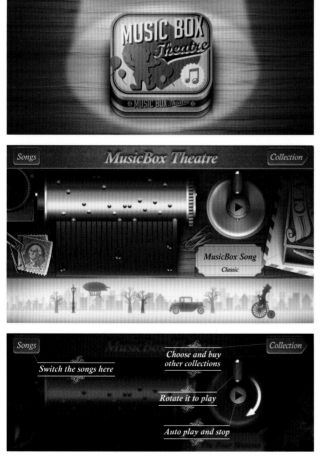

Switch the songs here

Choose and buy other collections

Rotate it to play

Auto play and stop

MusicBox Theatre

CHRISTMAS
1. Silent Night
2. Hark! The Herald Angels Sing
3. Joy to the World
4. The First Noël
5. Jingle Bells
6. The 12 days of Christmas

CLASSIC
1. Amazing Grace
2. Brahm's Lullaby
3. The Four Seasons, Spring
4. Swan Lake
5. The Blue Danube
6. Clair de Lune

CARNIVAL
1. Turkish March
2. William Tell
3. The Entertainer
4. Eine Kleine Nachtmusik
5. Maple Leaf Rag
6. 1812 Overture

Valentine
1. Canon In D Major
2. Carmen (Habanera)
3. Für Elise
4. Rêverie
5. Nocturne Op9, No.2
6. Ständchen (Schwanengesang)

Back

Swing iPhone Music App

The Swing iPhone Music App was inspired by the recent design trends. The designer created a minimalist and clean layout for Swing. He created a unique and cheerful experience for people who love music. He also attached particular importance to the images and typography to give the interface a modern look.

 Enes Danis

 MediaSona Digital Advertising Agency

 Turkey

 https://www.behance.net/enesdanis

Music Made by Art

The National Gallery of Denmark invited seven progressive musicians to create a piece of music based on their interpretations of a famous piece of art in the museum's collection. The musical interpretations were initially released one at a time but are now all available in the app that even allows users to listen to the music and enjoy the art piece, either at the museum or at home. Museum guests without smart phones can borrow a handheld device at the museum. The app is in Danish but given the limited amount of content, it should be possible for everyone to navigate and enjoy.

Jesper Winther

Uri Andersen & Jesper Winther

The National Gallery of Denmark

Denmark

www.umloud.dk

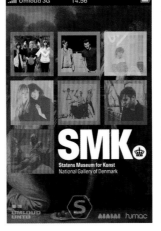

Amp App

Amp App is a music player for iPhone 5. The designer tried to make the GUI design as realistic as possible (skeuomorphic design), so the interface of the app was designed in the shape of a rock and roll guitar amplifier. The visual representation of a classical music item adds a vintage touch to the app.

 Tobia Crivellari

 Italy

 https://www.behance.net/my23

• AMP APP - UI Design - Wireframing

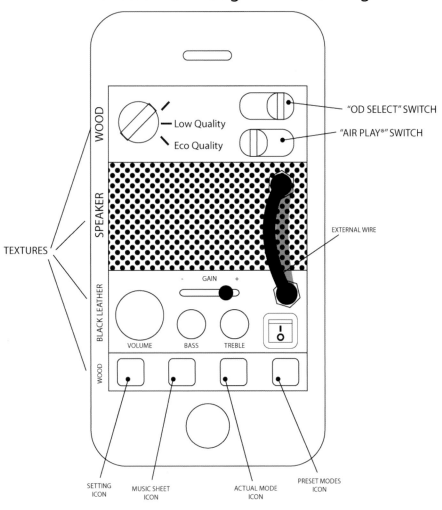

- "OD SELECT" SWITCH
- "AIR PLAY®" SWITCH
- EXTERNAL WIRE

WOOD

SPEAKER

BLACK LEATHER

WOOD

TEXTURES

Low Quality
Eco Quality

- GAIN +

VOLUME   BASS   TREBLE

SETTING ICON

MUSIC SHEET ICON

ACTUAL MODE ICON

PRESET MODES ICON

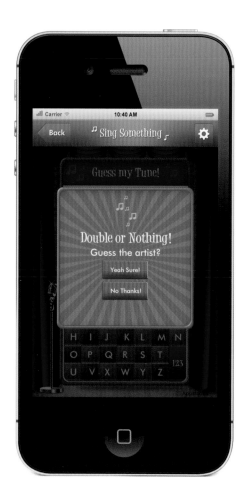

iSing Something

iSing Something is a game application suitable for people of all ages. Users can start a one-on-one challenge with their facebook friends by recording a song in their own voice and posting it for friends to guess the correct track name. The designer wanted to keep the design visually engaging for the users by emphasizing that they were the stars of the game. Continuing with that approach, the developers came up with the concept of a stage performance with curtains, spotlights and microphone as additional background decorations.

 Swati Verma

 AppStudioz Technologies Private Limited

 India

 www.appstudioz.com

Charito Mucha Marcha

This is an iPhone app for the Charito Mucha Marcha fashion brand. Users can make a Charito style photo using colorful elements provided in the app and then upload them to the official website of Charito Mucha Marcha. After that the photo can be posted on the blog of the site. In the app, the users can also find the brand's catalog, search the stores' locations and shop online.

 Esther Perez & Abraham Vivas

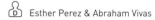 Moco Apps

 Charito Mucha Marcha

 Murcia, Spain

 http://www.moco-apps.com/

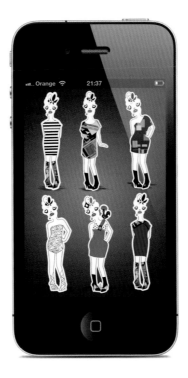

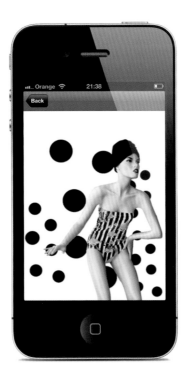

Camera Genius

This is a camera application which significantly increases standard functionality. It works on almost all Apple devices. It has separated focus and exposure areas, picture editing tools and effects, social network sharing feature and more. The interface for the iPhone is similar to a real DSLR camera.

 Eugene Cheporov

 Eugene Cheporov

 Artua LLC

 Codegoo

 USA

www.artua.com

PiCon–Photo Contests

PiCon is a photo application for mobile concept that can also provide a contest platform for shutterbugs. Users are able to post photos taken by the app to the active contests folders to participate in the photo contests and win prizes. By using filters, users can improve and personalize their photos. It is more appealing if there was an app not just for sharing photos and adding comments, but for getting something in return for taking part in the competition, such as special prizes, blog showcase and so on. Because of this, users are more likely to follow the contest progress and their own scores.

 Ilya Tsuprun

 Israel

 www.behance.net/icelanderus

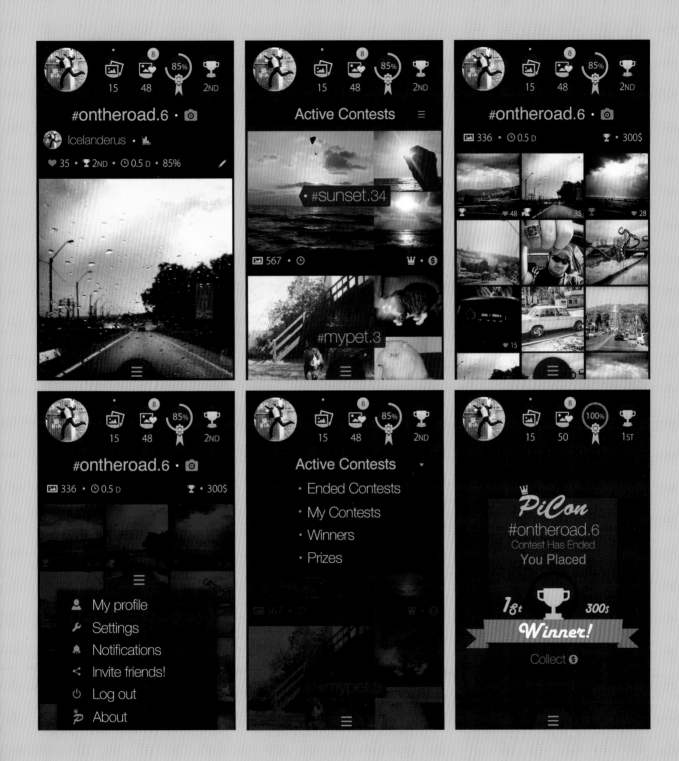

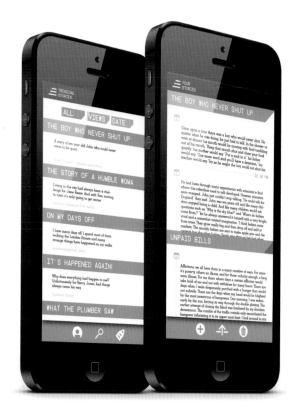

Fictitious

Fictitious is a conceptual app for writers, both professional and amateur. Users can slowly build up a story anytime anywhere using the app. Other users can read it and follow the development of the story, as well as make comments and share their own works. Once the story is finished, the writer can then publish it to the iBook store where the other users can download the articles. Green, the dominant hue of the user interface, helps to create a fresh and comfortable visual atmosphere for the readers.

 William Suckling

 Bayley Design

 United Kingdom

 behance.net/bayleydesign

1
2
3

4
5
6

7
8
9

10
11
12

1 App Icon
2 Comments
3 Mail
4 Add to Story
5 Upload Story
6 Date
7 View Story
8 Share Story
9 Delete
10 Profile
11 Search
12 Search Tags

Hollo

Hollo is a social app for people who love caves, designed to give cavers exactly what they need to learn about and explore caves. The term "hollo" is a transformation of the word "hello" to incorporate the social aspect of this app. It allows users to keep in touch and communicate with each other about cave tips, techniques, and discoveries. Users are able to utilize four main categories: profile, search/advanced search, toolbox and resources. With the rise in social network, this app gives the caving industry a unique app for users to stay tuned to the cave loving community.

 Shelby Lueckenotto

 United States

 www.behance.net/shelbylueckenotto

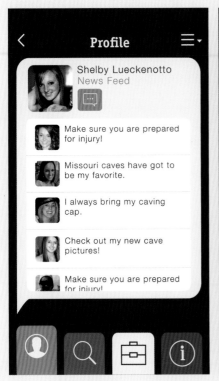

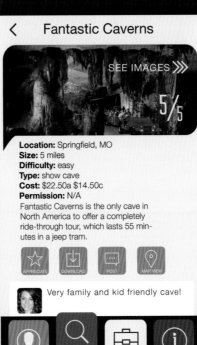

Profile App Concept

The Profile app concept is an app that collects users' all social network accounts on one platform. The designer's aim for the GUI design was to find a good combination of well-arranged UI elements that make the whole app easy to use. The matte, rubberlike interface was decorated with simple icons and subtle highlights.

 Martin David

 Germany

 www.srioz.com

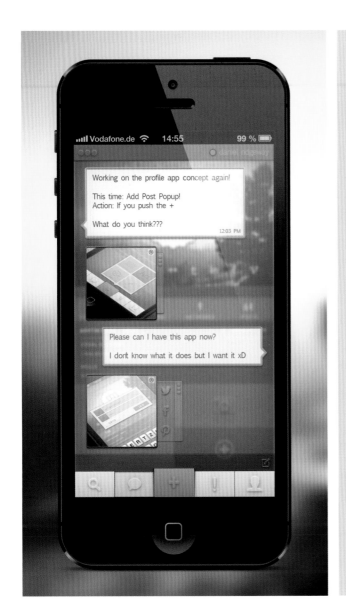

SHAPE   EMBOSS   SHADOW

TripUs

When spending time with friends on a trip, people might have a lot of things to do, like taking pictures, writing travel notes, updating facebook or tweeting. All that, plus traveling seems so tiring. This inspired the designer to create TripUs for organizing all these steps together and providing the user a good platform to share interesting things and beautiful pictures during the trip. The vertical arrangement of the sectors gives the user a legible vision.

Sittitsak Jiampotjaman

Thailand

http://www.stainfilm.com/

by Sittisuk Jiampojamarn, www.stainfilm.com

Şapka Çıkar

Yorum Yap

Derecelendir

Itiraf Et!

Itiraf Et! is a fun mobile application where people can make confessions, follow and comment on other users' confessions. Since the main subject is "confession", a dynamic and visually appealing interface was designed with the use of red color and the simplistic icons, which enable users to easily discover the application. Its menu is customizable according to the categories of the confessions like "relationships", "fears", "what if", etc. The witty "hats off to" button allows users to take hats off to the confessions they like. According to their participation, the users earn badges such as "the King Confessor". Itiraf Et! also engages the universities where the users' are able to select their university and use hash tags to give keywords about their confession topics. Itiraf Et! received the 1st Prize from the world's prestigious 7th Annual International Design Awards in Multimedia Interface Design Category.

 Onur Tatver

 Dilem Akıner

 Kraf&Co.

 Axoy Global

 Turkey

 www.kraf.co

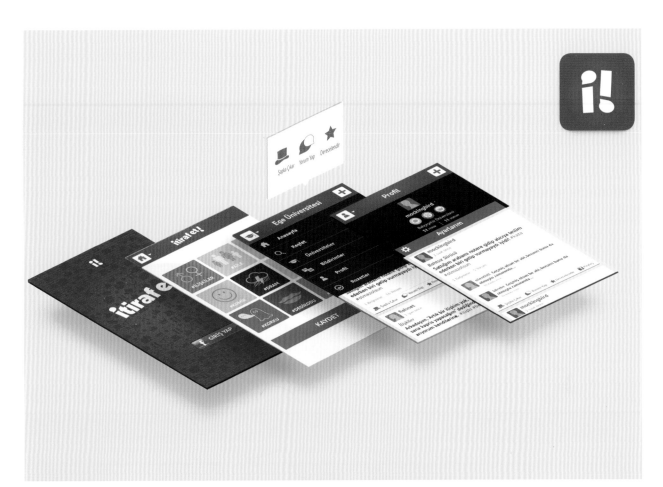

 Anasayfa

 KRAL İTİRAFÇI

 Şapka Çıkar

 #İLİŞKİLER | #AİLE | #OKUL

 Keşfet

ÇOK İTİRAF EDEN

 Yorum Yap

 Üniversiteler

ÇOK YORUM YAPAN

Derecelendir

#KOMİK | #DRAM | #KEŞKE

 Bildirimler

 İTİRAF BEĞENEN

Kadın Profil

#KORKU | #DEDİKODU | #FİKİRVER

 Profil

ÇOK İTİRAF OKUYAN

Erkek Profil

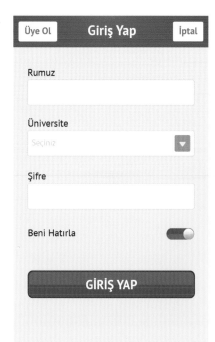

MobilFinder

Nowadays some people seem to go crazy if they cannot find their phones. So the designer had the idea to create an app to find the lost phone. With this app, the owner only has to call out for the phone by asking: "Where are you?" The phone reacts automatically and when the switch is on, the phone can "listen" to the user's voice. With the timer the user can set active periods for the app to be on in order to save the battery life. The concept is simple and the interface has no unnecessary or complicated decorations. There is a basic on/off button and a timer.

 Laszlo Svajer

 Zoltan Gabor Nagy

 Mobil Weekend - Application Creator Contest, Mickolc, Hungary

 Hungary

 www.esgraphic.hu

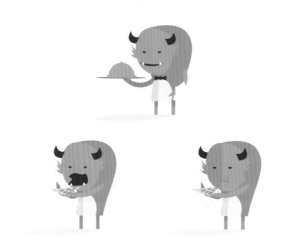

Lunch Hunch

Lunch Hunch is an app that helps users to make lunch choices. One user acts as the group leader and chooses 3 menu items and 3 restaurants based on those menu items. The leader then invites a group of coworkers or friends, with these three choices. The friends vote on the choices and the majority wins. A "lunch hunch" is "served" at the end.

Camille Woods

Camille Woods

USA

Camillewoodsdesign.com

LUNCH HUNCH

My Cookmarks

My Cookmarks is aimed at all ambitious cooks who want to spend more time cooking and less time searching. Lots of apps try to make the cook's familiar cookbooks redundant. But is that really what people want? The approach of this project is different. A smartphone app was developed which not only archives favorite recipes in a simple way, but also makes it easy to find. Finding that particular recipe has never been easier. The clear design and the intuitive, user-friendly operation eliminate all unnecessary information. The result is a fine balance of functionality and design.

 les pals

 les pals

Berlin Germany

 www.lespals.de

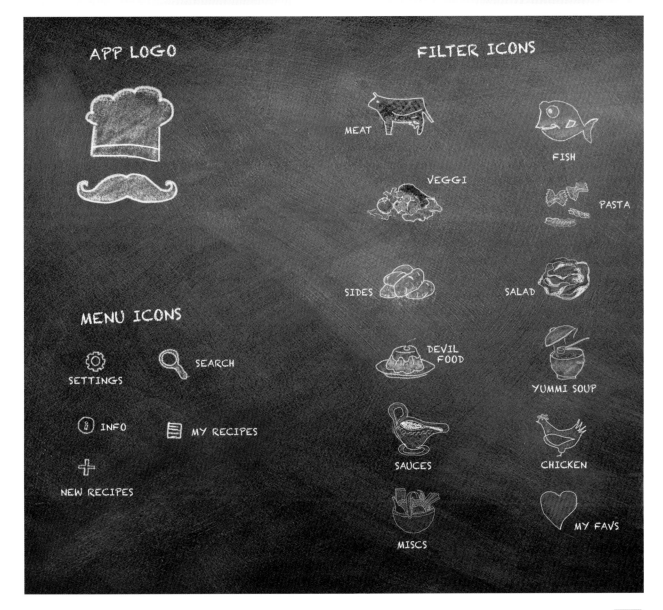

Sweety App

Sweety is a recipe app for cupcakes. Users can learn how to make different kinds of cupcakes, as well as where to buy their favorite cupcakes nearby with detailed directions from the app. The designer used attractive cupcake colors and a vintage style to convey an artistic look for the design.

 Sherif Ahmed Shaaban

 N&Y

 Egypt

 www.be.net/sherif-shaaban

Screen 1 — Shopping

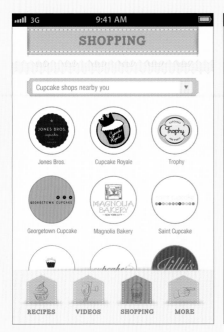

SHOPPING

Cupcake shops nearby you ▼

Jones Bros. Cupcake Royale Trophy

Georgetown Cupcake Magnolia Bakery Saint Cupcake

RECIPES VIDEOS SHOPPING MORE

Screen 2 — Videos

VIDEOS

Star Cupcake Colorful Cupcake

Golden Cupcake Cinstars Cupcake

Cherry Cupcake Pink tart Cupcake

RECIPES VIDEOS SHOPPING MORE

Screen 3 — Recipes

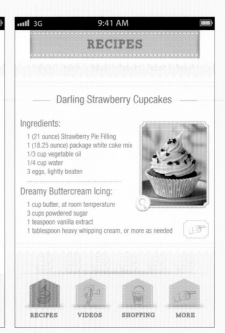

RECIPES

Darling Strawberry Cupcakes

Ingredients:
1 (21 ounce) Strawberry Pie Filling
1 (18.25 ounce) package white cake mix
1/3 cup vegetable oil
1/4 cup water
3 eggs, lightly beaten

Dreamy Buttercream Icing:
1 cup butter, at room temperature
3 cups powdered sugar
1 teaspoon vanilla extract
1 tablespoon heavy whipping cream, or more as needed

RECIPES VIDEOS SHOPPING MORE

Logo

Sweety
Delicious Cupcakes

Icons

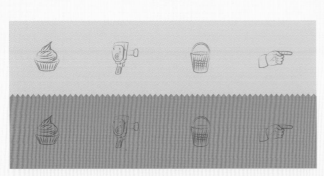

Screen 4 — Recipes

RECIPES

GOURMET CUPCAKE

RECIPES VIDEOS SHOPPING MORE

Coffee Ordering

This design is an app for ordering coffee on-the-go. The designer saw the time constraints of the users to be the major concern. To that end, the designer included two additional options to the standard process for mobile ordering, which is similar to ordering online.

 Michael Novoselov

 Israel

 http://mengel.prosite.com/

The two time-saving options that the designer added are:

1. The option of delivery: one can either pick-up pre-ordered coffee or have it delivered to the designated address.

2. The option of favorites: if one drinks the same coffee every morning, it would be just a single click to place the order.

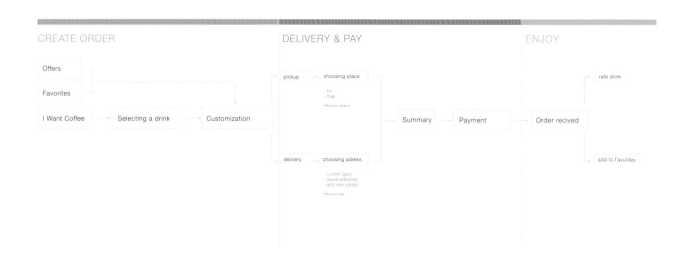

ENJOY

Offers

Favorites

I Want Coffee → Selecting a drink → Customization

pickup → choosing place
- list
- map
*filtering by distance

delivery → choosing adress
- current (gps)
- saved adresses
- add new adress
*filtering by time

Summary → Payment → Order recived

rate drink

add to Favorites

Dynamic Order status on dashboard

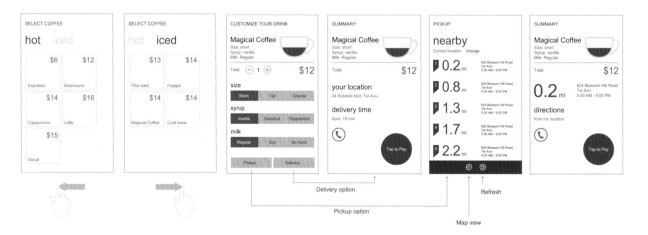

Delivery option

Pickup option

Refresh

Map view

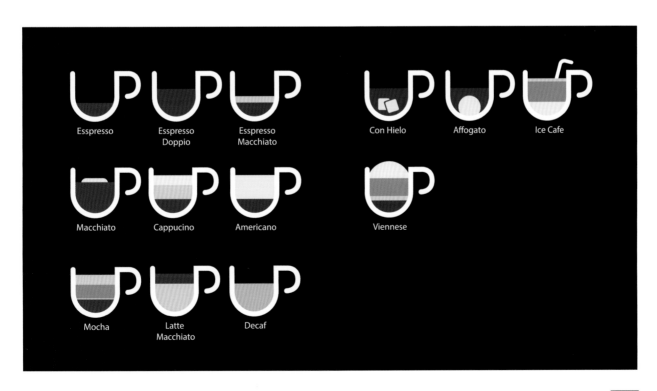

Spirit Test

The designers of this app wanted to create a simple and playful app that allows people to monitor their consumption of alcoholic beverages. They first defined a framework that included all stages, so that the app would be attractive and extremely simple to use. They selected interface elements that were already offered in the Apple library and that were used in many apps.

This design is reminiscent of an atmosphere that is familiar to people who drink, and conveys the idea of "drinking responsibly". It meets the standards of the brands that are owned by Spirit Suisse and the values that this organization promotes.

 Agathe Altwegg

 Pascal Wicht

 ENIGMA Productions Sàrl

 Spirit Suisse

 Switzerland

 enigmaprod.ch

I'm Hungry!

Research into brand relationships and neuromarketing led to an application designed to tell the user what can be eaten based on his/her emotions. The app utilizes the emotion, action and reward system of habit building to simplify the decision-making process of grocery shopping. Interface elements change based on the phone's internal clock.

Laurel Ames

USA

lamesdesign.com

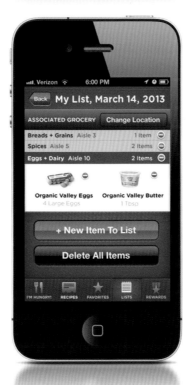

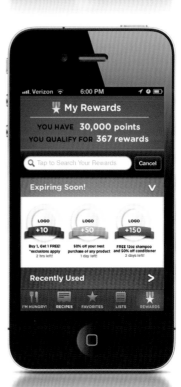

Ringmaster

Ringmaster is a touch screen app that helps parents and their children to maintain healthy lifestyle. Ringmaster is designed for the parents to input data, planning for their children, while the children could view and keep track of their daily data. The children can then get into the habit of arranging their time to balance study and fun. The app has five main categories: Sleep, Play, Clean, Eat, and Work. The app's setting categories include: Edit Account, Daily Report, and Savings.

 Soo Yeun Ji, Jane Brown, Olivia Luo, Amenda Kim

 USA

 jisooyeunji.com

MONSTER   BOY   GIRL   ANIMAL

Sleep   Play   Clean   Eat   Work

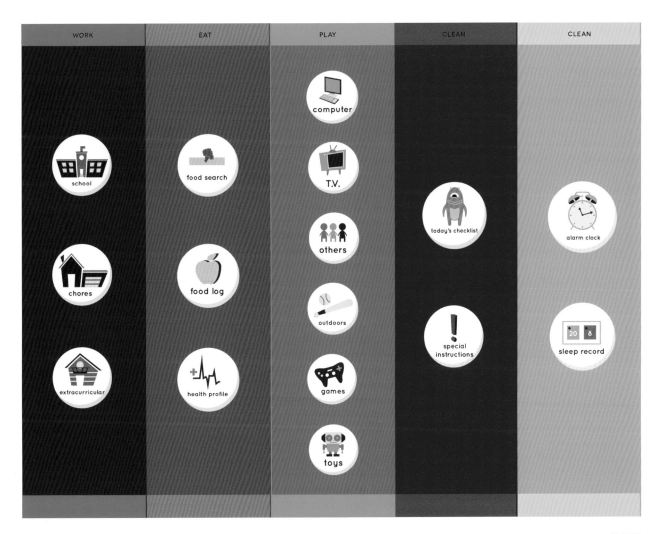

WORK	EAT	PLAY	CLEAN	CLEAN
		computer		
school	food search	T.V.		alarm clock
		others	today's checklist	
chores	food log	outdoors		sleep record
		games	special instructions	
extracurricular	health profile	toys		

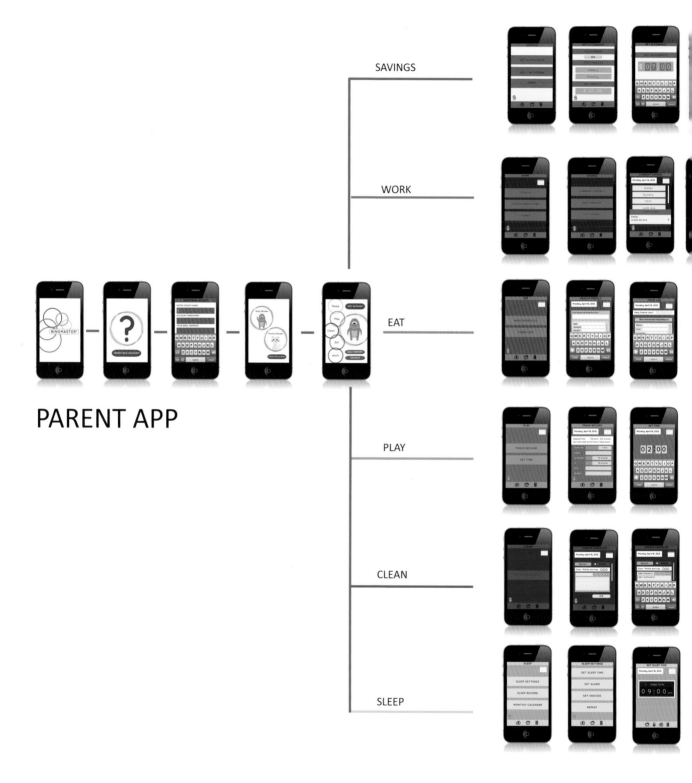

PARENT APP

SAVINGS

WORK

EAT

PLAY

CLEAN

SLEEP

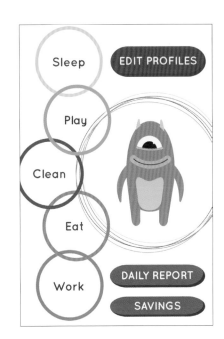

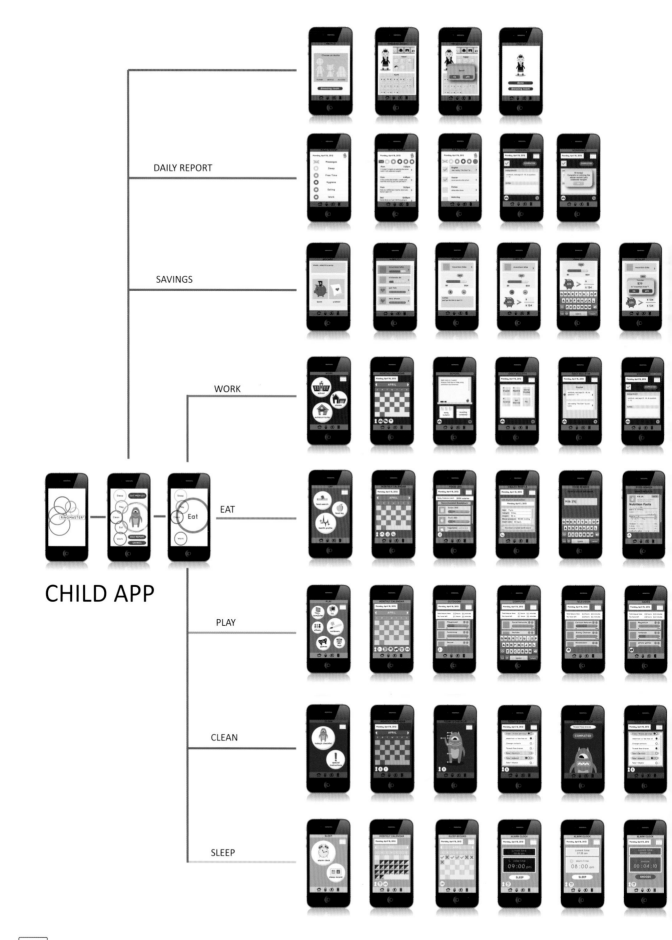

DAILY REPORT

SAVINGS

WORK

EAT

CHILD APP

PLAY

CLEAN

SLEEP

SAVINGS

mom added $5 to savings

bank   wishlist

WORKSPACE

Monday, April 16, 2012

✓   COMPLETED

assignment:

workbook, read page 20 - 40, do questions
1 - 10

notes:

PLAY

computer   T.V.

others   outdoors

games   toys

TODAY'S CHECKLIST

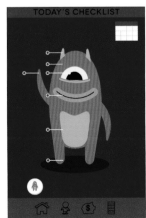

DRESSING ROOM

head

eyes

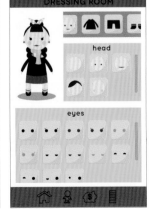

MONTHLY CALENDAR

Monday, April 16, 2012

◀   APRIL   ▶

S M T W T F S

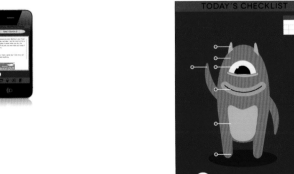

The Whispering House

This project was specially designed to create a more effective method of communication between a house and its absent owner. The house is given a "voice" in the app so it can "speak" to its owner via status messages. This provides constant access so that the owner knows what is going on at home and is able to react rapidly on unexpected incidents. The home screen of the app gives an overview about all messages reported by the user's house. Important information and problems which have to be solved urgently are highlighted and will pop up on the smartphone's home screen. Accessing to the internet and building a completely linked status to the house are the main requirements for the app.

Kebrina Urbaniak

Germany

https://www.behance.net/KebrinaUrbaniak

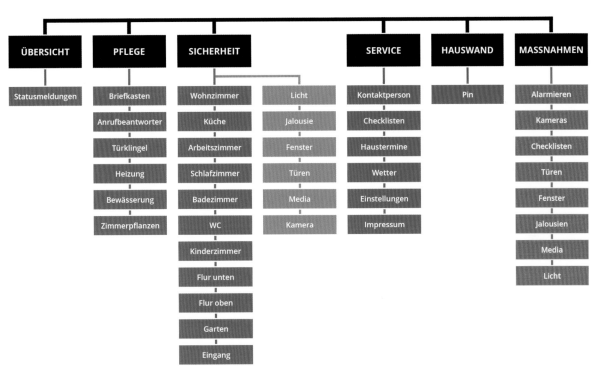

ÜBERSICHT	PFLEGE	SICHERHEIT		SERVICE	HAUSWAND	MASSNAHMEN
Statusmeldungen	Briefkasten	Wohnzimmer	Licht	Kontaktperson	Pin	Alarmieren
	Anrufbeantworter	Küche	Jalousie	Checklisten		Kameras
	Türklingel	Arbeitszimmer	Fenster	Haustermine		Checklisten
	Heizung	Schlafzimmer	Türen	Wetter		Türen
	Bewässerung	Badezimmer	Media	Einstellungen		Fenster
	Zimmerpflanzen	WC	Kamera	Impressum		Jalousien
		Kinderzimmer				Media
		Flur unten				Licht
		Flur oben				
		Garten				
		Eingang				

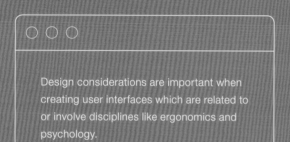

Design considerations are important when creating user interfaces which are related to or involve disciplines like ergonomics and psychology.

While it can be difficult to anticipate every need, it is possible to offer some alternatives and build a bit of flexibility into the design of your resource.

Effectiveness, efficiency and satisfaction are important factors to consider when evaluating your GUI and usability. Experts have developed several approaches to measure these, including:

1. Usability testing with real users.

2. Usability evaluations by the designer (potentially you) or other experts.

3. Gathering user feedback.

4. Usage logging.

To deliver desired functionality without starting from scratch, spending a fortune or risking "reinventing the wheel", you can simply use off-the-shelf systems that are sufficiently flexible for experienced programmers to customize the GUI, or develop their own interfaces.

Some producers will also supply highly customized systems for their clients, using a mix of existing modules and new components to create a project that is a good fit for users' needs.

The graphical user interface is one of the most important parts of any program because it determines how easily you can make the program do what you want.

If you're developing your own GUI, accessibility is best addressed as part of the design process, rather than dealt with as an afterthought or an add-on.

It is vital to study what others have done. Take the time to locate and assess other digital media collections. Look closely at those that are similar to your own, but also observe a wider field, considering what is happening within other sectors and in other countries.

Instead of hastily changing your interface in response to a request or a complaint, you should be proactive in providing a resource that offers the best possible experience to the widest possible audience.

Meow

The mobile theme Meow designed for the GO Launcher of the Android market was intended to capture the hearts of cat lovers with its feline-centric design. The design style is pleasant, while the striking colors created a fresh and lively atmosphere. A distinctive icon design captures the characteristics of cats that many feline lovers appreciate. In the Twitter icon, for example, the cat's paws are reaching out for a runaway bird, which creates an interesting scene.

 April Chen

 China

 www.behance.net/aprilchen

meow

 Contact
 Phone
 Message
 Browser
 Music
 Setting

 Mail
 Gmail
 Store
 Map
 Skype
 Calculator

 Camera
 Gallery
 Clock
 Twitter
 Facebook
 Download

 Canlendar
 YouTube
 GoWeather
 GameCenter
 Go Backup
 Go Lock

161

Meow Weather
by April Chen

 HONGKONG ›
02:14 AM
31°C Sunny ↻
28°35°, Wind : VAR 2 mph · 2/06/2013 Mon.

 HONGKONG ›
22:29 PM
26°C Sunny ↻
21°28°, Wind : VAR 2 mph · 2/06/2013 Mon.

 HONGKONG ›
04:38 AM
24°C Overcast ↻
18°26°, Wind : VAR 2 mph · 2/06/2013 Mon.

 HONGKONG ›
02:30 AM
24°C Cloudy ↻
15°28°, Wind : VAR 2 mph · 2/06/2013 Mon.

 HONGKONG ›
21:33 PM
19°C Cloudy ↻
11°19°, Wind : VAR 2 mph · 2/06/2013 Mon.

 HONGKONG ›
06:33 AM
12°C Foggy ↻
11°18°, Wind : VAR 2 mph · 2/06/2013 Mon.

 HONGKONG ›
05:29 AM
15°C Storm ↻
15°18°, Wind : VAR 2 mph · 2/06/2013 Mon.

 HONGKONG ›
18:31 AM
17°C Rainy ↻
11°19°, Wind : VAR 2 mph · 2/06/2013 Mon.

 HONGKONG ›
05:29 AM
-5°C Snowy ↻
-5°8°, Wind : VAR 2 mph · 2/06/2013 Mon.

 HONGKONG ›
19:45 AM
32°C Unknown ↻
11°19°, Wind : VAR 2 mph · 2/06/2013 Mon.

↻ °C °F

0123456789

 Sunny

 Clear Night

 Cloudy

 Cloudy Night

Overcast

 Rainy

 Storm

 Snowy

Foggy

 Unknown

↻ °C °F

0123456789

 HONGKONG ›
05:29 AM
-5°C Snowy ↻
-5°/8°, Wind : VAR 2 mph · 2/06/2013 Mon.

Pirate Era

The mobile theme Pirate Era was designed for the GO Launcher of Android. The designer used a pirate for the motif, while sailing the ocean was the theme. The light blue background was meant to relax the user. Although pirate themes are often approached in a masculine style, the colorful and lovely graphic design may prove to be very attractive to women. All the patterns and icons were designed in a cartoon style so that the fearsome image of a pirate was transformed into something cute.

 April Chen

 China

 www.behance.net/aprilchen

PIRATE ERA

Pirate Era • Weather

By April Chen

SIDNEY› Sunny 2/06/2013 Mon.	31°C 28°35°	
SIDNEY› Clear sky 2/06/2013 Mon.	26°C 28°35°	
SIDNEY› Cloudy 2/06/2013 Mon.	21°C 21°35°	
SIDNEY› Overcast 2/06/2013 Mon.	32°C 28°35°	
SIDNEY› Clear sky 2/06/2013 Mon.	26°C 28°35°	
SIDNEY› Foggy 2/06/2013 Mon.	12°C 10°16°	
SIDNEY› Rainy 2/06/2013 Mon.	22°C 21°35°	
SIDNEY› Rainy 2/06/2013 Mon.	22°C 21°35°	
SIDNEY› Snowy 2/06/2013 Mon.	-6°C -8°4°	

SIDNEY› Unknown 2/06/2013 Mon. 15°C 10°16°

°C °F › ↻
1234567890

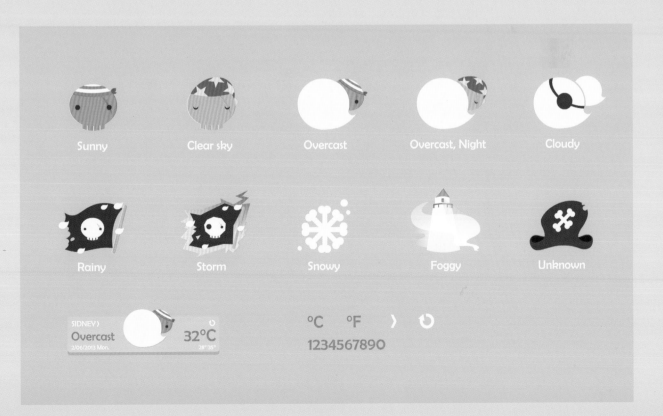

Sunny Clear sky Overcast Overcast, Night Cloudy

Rainy Storm Snowy Foggy Unknown

SIDNEY› Overcast 2/06/2013 Mon. 32°C 28°35°

°C °F › ↻
1234567890

Snowman

Snowman is a mobile phone theme designed for the GO Launcher of Android. The doodle style brings liveliness to the interface design.

 April Chen

 China

 www.behance.net/aprilchen

Minimalist Icons

Disregarding the often utilized skeuomorphic method, this project was designed to strip the iPhone homescreen of amateur color schemes and unnecessary shapes, replacing them with beautiful icons created using a modified version of Apples' own grid.

This concept is strictly for advanced users who are comfortable with their interface layout and no longer need bold reminders as to where buttons are, and for those who wish to opt for something more stylish and sleek.

Zack O'Toole

England

www.zackotoole.com

Soft Sweets

Maintaining the recognizability and usability of conventional icons for weather forecast, this app adopted a special icon set. The puffy "sweets" with different flavors showcase different weather conditions. And the external interface was turned into "candy bags" accordingly.

 Busywait (Huang lin)

 Weather Reader

 China

www.busywait.net

Smartphone Icon Sets

The focus of this project is a graphic concept for a recognizable and user-friendly icon set. The designer created a new interface different from the complexity of some GUIs presently on the market. The apps have been categorized into three main areas, each one with a different color, in a fully customizable GUI. Location, names and colors can be changed by the user.

The areas of interest are accessible from the main screen. There is also a fourth area which allows the user to display all the apps downloaded on the smartphone. You can access the four main areas using directional movements on the screen (top, bottom, left and right) that are each associated with a specific macro-area.

Stefania Pizzichi

Italy

 www.stefaniapizzichi.it

The designer of this app developed two themes for the same interface:

• One-line theme: basic and intuitive graphics, with a serious and practical design thought for a sports loving and technologically up-to-date male target.

• Kawaii theme: playful, pastel colored with icons designed for an imaginative and cheerful female target market.

Electric Tourbillon Home Screen UI

Electric Tourbillon Home Screen is a user interface for information aggregation. The designer integrated social functions and apps which are often used together, such as the Clock, Phone, Contact, Weather, Email, SMS and so on. In this case, users could manage their life and check the social messages intuitively. One of the inspirations came from the classic mechanism of the tourbillon which represents eternity and time. And the famous movie Tron has also inspired the designer with its strong "Electro" style. He utilized the classics as well as technology for the theme of the design so as to create a combination of the mechanical and the electronic.

 Xiwen Huang

 GO Launcher

 China

 www.behance.net/kevinG

○ Classical & Nostalgic

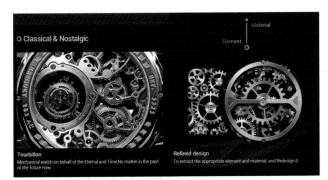

Material

Element

Tourbillon
Mechanical watch on behalf of the Eternal and Time,No matter in the past or the future now.

Refined design
To extract the appropriate element and material, and Redesign it.

○ Classical & Music

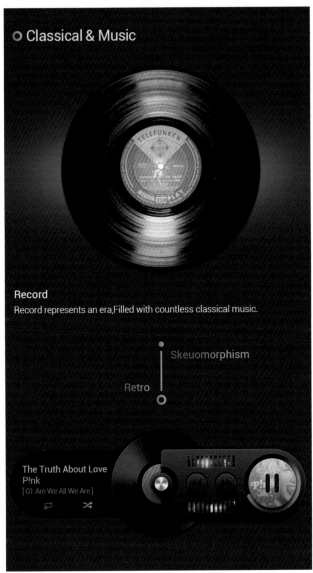

Record
Record represents an era,Filled with countless classical music.

Skeuomorphism

Retro

The Truth About Love
P!nk
[01 Are We All We Are]

Icon idea
Science and technology progress over time,TRON 2010 is a example of the integration of classical and technology.

Colour

Cycle

26°
LONDON
SUNNY

23   70   92

When talking about the classics, people often point to vinyl records since they stand for a generation of great music. The designer made it possible to inherit the classic by digitizing music from vinyl records.

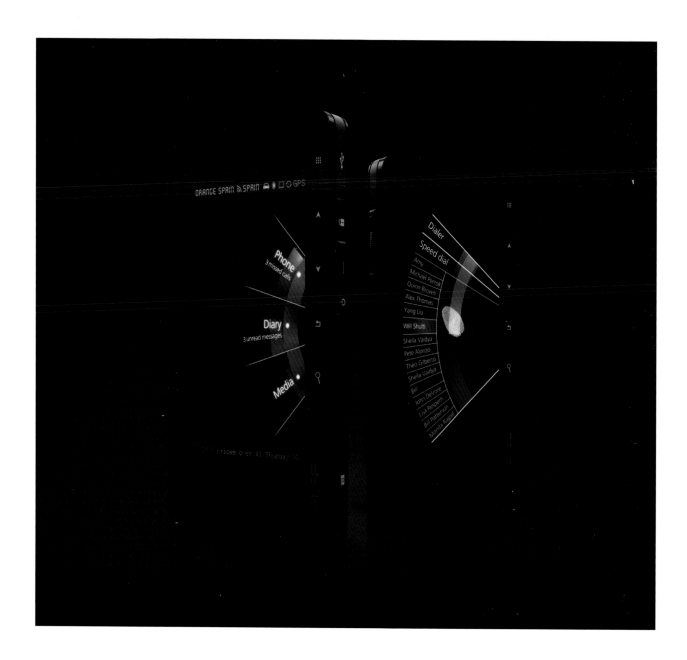

Else Mobile

In designing the user experience for First Else, the designers sought to implement common ideas on how the future would look like in a tangible, real life product. The design was inspired by a number of elements in both the human-made and natural resources in the world around us. Among them are Stanley Kubrick's Space Odyssey, Batman, the view of earth from space, water ripples, iceberg layers and luminous underwater creatures.

Yael Burstein, Ori Succary, Ronen Shaya, Noa Dolberg, Liron Damir, Natali Kravitz, Erez Bar, Alisa Goikhman, Shachar Brill, Ohad Elimelech, Alon Feuirstein, Itai Vonshak, Alex Rapapport, Dana Dumai, Liron Marcus Jacobi, Itay Levin & Eli Reifman.

Ori Succary

Succary Inc.

Emblaze Mobile

Israel

www.succary.com

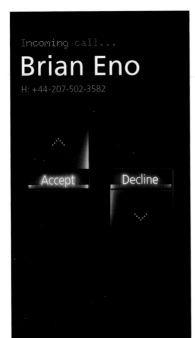

Incoming call...

Brian Eno

H: +44-207-502-3582

Accept   Decline

Jerusalem
GMT +2

22:40

1/12/2008
click to set

06:32
Sunrise

18:33
Sunset

① 9.30 once   (in 9 hours)
② 11.35 Everyday   (in 11 hours)
③ Add Alarm

Done

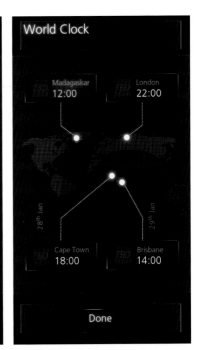

World Clock

Madagaskar
12:00

London
22:00

Cape Town
18:00

Brisbane
14:00

28th Jan   29th Jan

Done

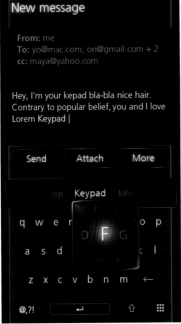

New message

From: me
To: yo@mac.com; ori@gmail.com + 2
cc: maya@yahoo.com

Hey, I'm your kepad bla-bla nice hair.
Contrary to popular belief, you and I love
Lorem Keypad |

Send   Attach   More

Keypad

q w e r   o p
a s d   l
z x c v b n m ←

@,?!   ⟵   ⇧   ⊞

Contact list

Betty Bluz
Rob Mob
Jhonathan quarny
Yaron cox
Eli yaspan

Send   More   C

1	2 abc	3 def
4 ghi	5 jkl	6 mno
7 pqrs	8 tuv	9 wxyz
*	0	#

Speed Dialer | Speed SMS

GPSLBS
Map Only

New York
Manhattan

Search   Where to   More

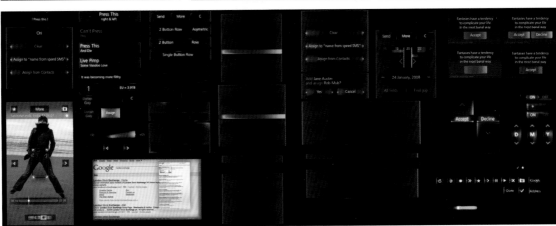

Vine for Windows Phone

Vine is a mobile app owned by Twitter that enables its users to create and post short video clips with a maximum clip length of six seconds. With the popularity of the app for the iOS and Android systems, the designer decided to create his own concept for the Windows Phone. He referenced to the Vine App for iOS but also changed some things in his own style.

 Victor Berbel

 Brazil

 www.v89.me
behance.net/victorberbel

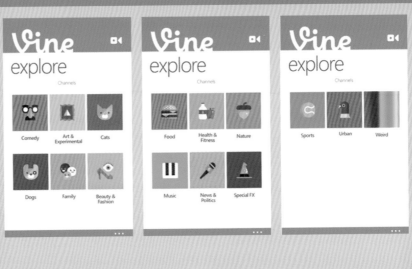

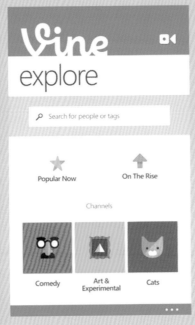

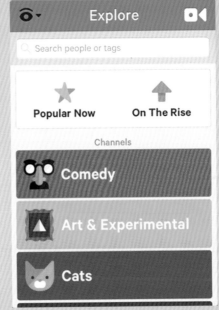

Windows Phone

iOS

Blue Velvet UI Kit

Blue Velvet is a complete, highly detailed and user-friendly template for Android based phones in PSD format. It contains several ready-to-use views and a UI Kit with over 100 elements. It also contains a set of 3 actions for quick and easy resizing.

 Matias Pablo Gallipoli

Argentina

 matiasgallipoli.com

HEADER STYLES

Blue Velvet

Blue Velvet

Search...

Blue Velvet

Blue Velvet

Search...

2 selected

HEADER ELEMENTS

0   2

TOOLBAR STYLES

Send

LIST STYLES

Single Line item

Two Line Item
this is the second line

Two Line Item
with avatar

Single Line item

Two Line Item
this is the second line

Two Line Item
with avatar

PROFILE HEADER

BACKGROUNDS

MENU STYLES

SINGLE COLUMN BLOCKS

Quince
Upscale
Californian-Italian...

Kokkari Estiatorio

Bix

GRID BLOCKS

Storage   Games   Music

Pictures   Calendar   Notes

Camera   Chat   Maps

PANEL STYLES

UI ELEMENTS

Tab one   Tab two   Tab three

Normal

Pressed

Disabled

OFF   OFF   9   102

ON   ON   76   1256

Today 14:56 PM

ICONS

"I have a keen eye for details and to be honest I'm quite obsessive about it."

Heavenly GUI Kit Elements

This GUI kit contains the basic elements of web design, which can be used in the development of sites, blogs and other web pages. With these elements, designers can save a lot of time when creating the basic design of user interfaces. All items are made in the same style with sky blue for the primary theme.

 Radmir Mingaliev

 Russia

 http://ramimcm.in/

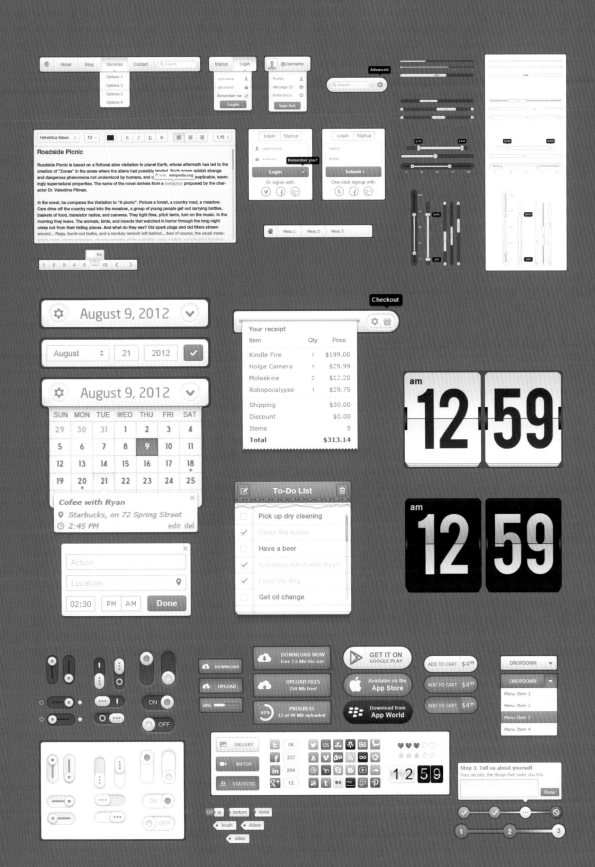

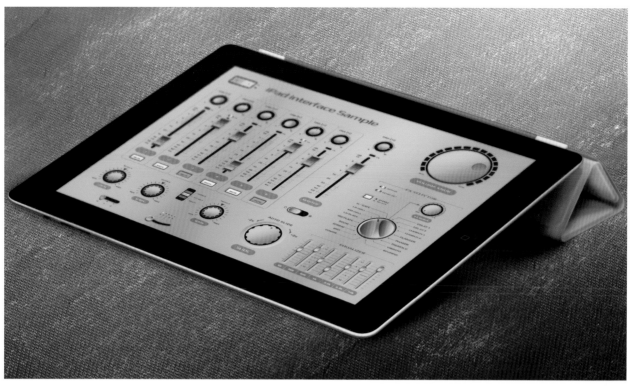

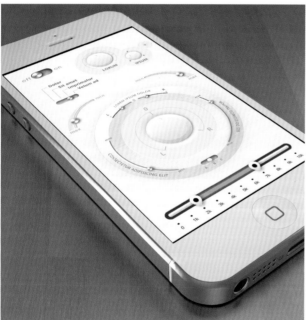

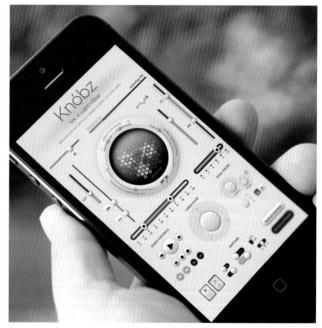

Knóbz Vol.5

Knóbz Vol.5 is a set of GUI elements for applications and websites. It contains full vector Photoshop layers and shapes organized into well named layer groups. There are two versions: one for regular desktop apps (72 ppi) and one for Retina/HDPI apps (326 ppi).

 Alexey Kolpikov

 Kolpikov.ru

 Russia

 https://www.linkedin.com/in/despoth

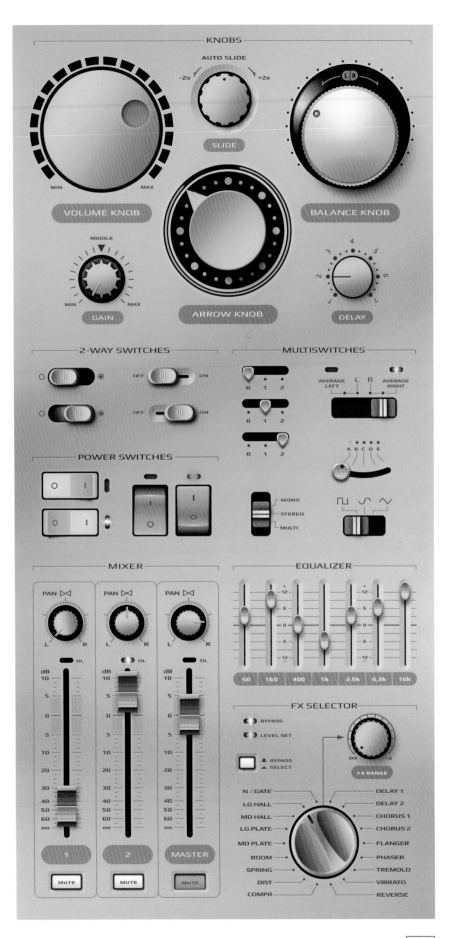

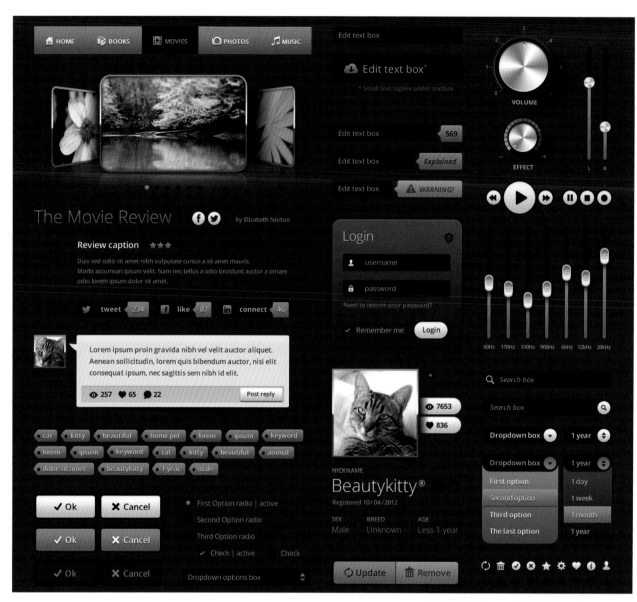

Ruthenium GUI Kit

The full version of the Ruthenium GUI Kit includes over 200 objects. It is a massive collection of GUI objects for desktop/mobile apps and web design. This huge set includes generic and unique controls for any kind of application and website.

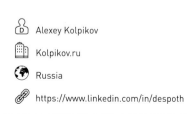

Alexey Kolpikov

Kolpikov.ru

Russia

https://www.linkedin.com/in/despoth

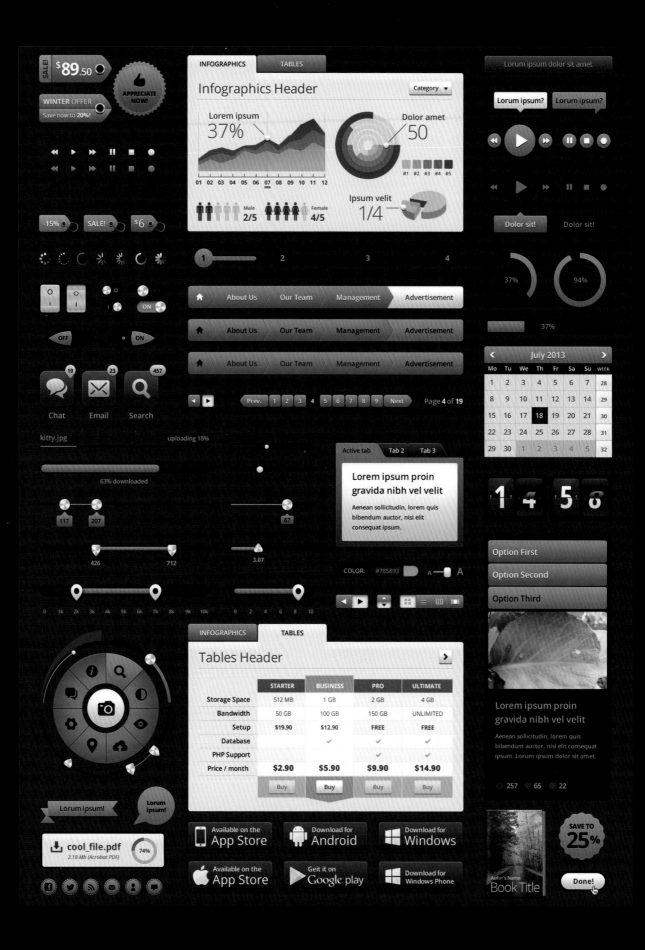

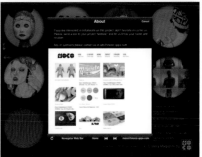

O Gallery 1

O Gallery is a new concept of contemporary art diffusion. It's an interactive space where you can experience the selected work of great artists of graphic design, illustration, typography, music, painting, photography, sculpture, video art and everything you can figure out concerning the artistic world, in one single spot.

O Gallery 1 is the first of a series of interactive Apps for iPad.

 Esther Perez & Abraham Vivas

 Murcia, Spain

www.moco-apps.com

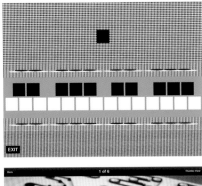

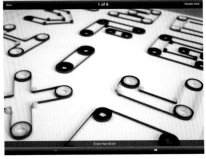

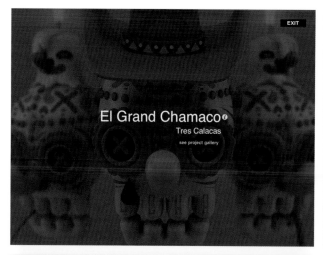

El Grand Chamaco *i*

Tres Calacas

see project gallery

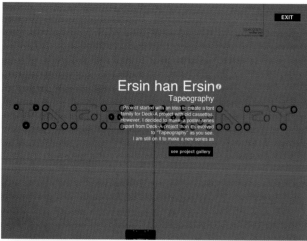

Ersin han Ersin *i*

Tapeography

Project started with an idea to create a font
family for Deck-A project with old cassettes.
However, I decided to make a poster series
apart from Deck-A project than it's evolved
to "Tapeography" as you see.
I am still on it to make a new series as

see project gallery

see project gallery

About   Cancel

Nina Nolte

Contact
Nina Nolte
Location
Dusseldorf - Germany
Send Mail

Nina Nolte was born in 1957 in El Salvador and grew up in Germany and
Spain. Whilst employed in a German company Nina Nolte pursued her
passion for painting and had her first solo show in 1991. She has since
exhibited internationally in galleries and art fairs. Nina Nolte lived in Malaga
for fifteen years before moving to Dusseldorf in 2011.

www.ninanolte.com

Maleonn's photo studio

Cousin Mary, acrylic on canvas, 100x160cm

El Grand Chamaco

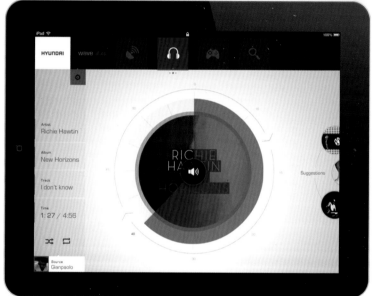

Wave iPad App

Wave is an application designed for iPad and iPhone to be used in a car. Today, the interior of a car is becoming more like a living space, which means a constant change of user needs.

The application consists of 3 different macro areas related to music:

1. Car Passengers as a Micro-Community

The car owner can change the settings of this application and turn his device into a Hub. Via Bluetooth, the Hub is capable to detect all the other passengers' devices and create an automatic playlist based on all the music archives stored in different devices.

Gianpaolo Tucci, LBI Italy (agency)

Hyundai contest

Italy

www.gianpaolotucci.com

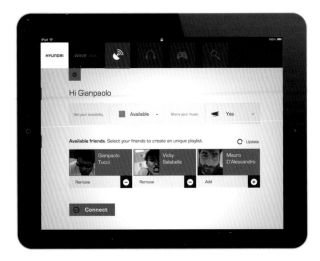

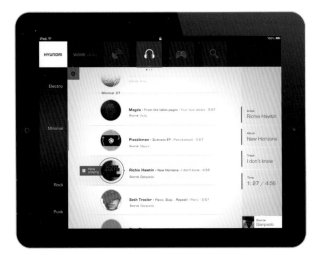

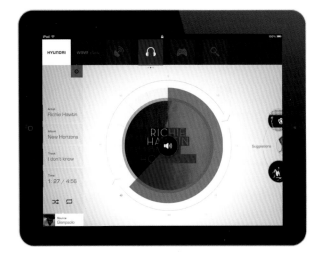

wave object's status ıllıılıılı

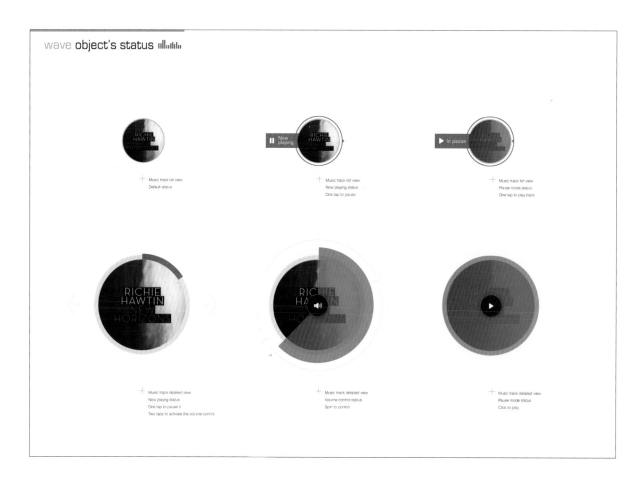

wave layout structure ıllıılıılı

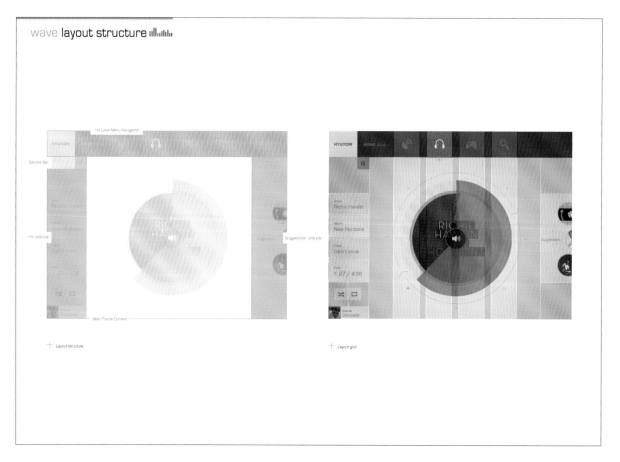

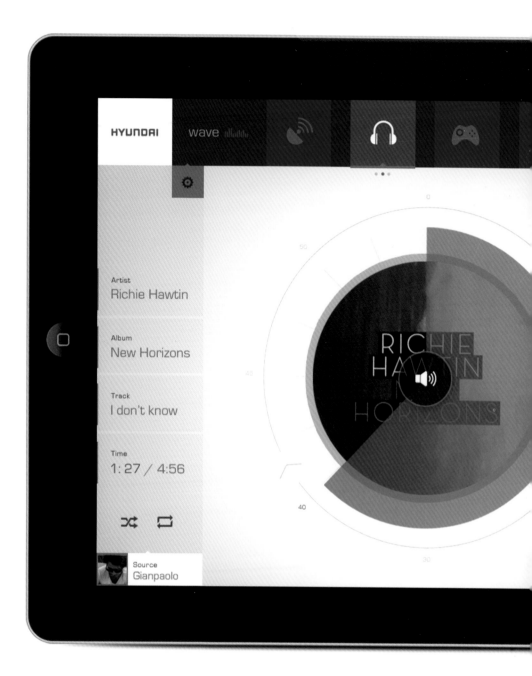

2. Different Micro-Communities form a Macro-Community

There are push notifications about songs from nearby driver's instant listening. Users can choose to listen to the same song or even browse others' playlists.

3. Proper Driving Behavior through Music

With a GPS, the application can detect the speed limit of the street which you are driving in. Whenever you are overspeed, the music will slow down automatically.

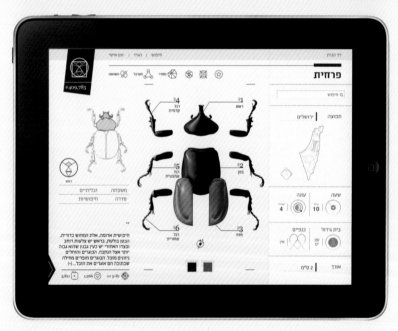

Insect Definer

Insect Definer is a content application for iPad, which allows digital text reading with a transformation from printed content to digital media. The app will allow exploring and experiencing insects' world in a new interactive way. The core of the app is its search capabilities. It uses creative search values that the printed book cannot provide us with. Using this new way of exploring, new intersections and contexts in nature will be revealed between different insects.

 Yael Cohen

 Israel

 www.yaelco.com

גל סיני

צילומים   סטטיסטיקה

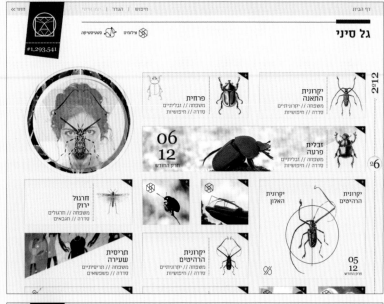

2 מ12

6 מ

יקרונית התאנה
משפחה // יקרוניתיים
סדרה // חיפושיות

פרחית
משפחה // זבליתיים
סדרה // חיפושיות

זבלית פרעה
משפחה // זבליתיים
סדרה // חיפושיות

06 12
חזיק החודש

יקרונית הרהיטים
משפחה // יקרוניתיים
סדרה // חיפושיות

יקרונית האלון

חרגול ירוק
משפחה // חרגולים
סדרה // חגבאים

05 12
חזיק החודש

תריסית שעירה
משפחה // תריסיתיים
סדרה // פשפשאים

יקרונית הרהיטים
משפחה // יקרוניתיים
סדרה // חיפושיות

השוואה

תרומי

חיפוש

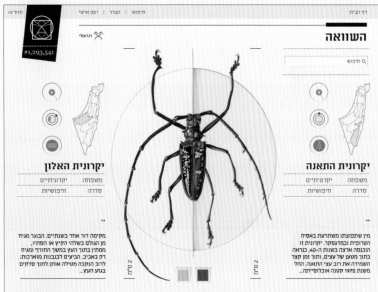

יקרונית האלון

משפחה	יקרוניתיים
סדרה	חיפושיות

**

מקימה דור אחד בשנתיים. הבוגר מגיח
מן הגולם בשלהי הקיץ או הסתיו,
מתחיו בתוך העץ במשך החורף ומגיח
ריק באביב. הביצים לבגבנות מוארכות.
לרוב הנקבה מטילה אותן לתוך סדקים
בגזע העץ...

2 ס"מ

יקרונית התאנה

משפחה	יקרוניתיים
סדרה	חיפושיות

**

מין שתפוצתו משתרעת באסיה
הטרופית ובמדגסקר. יקרונית זו
הוכנסה ארצה בשנות ה-40, בגראה
בתוך מצעו של עצים, ותוך זמן קצר
השמידה את רוב עצי התאנה. החל
משנת 1970 קטנה אוכלוסייתה...

2 ס"מ

מערבל

תרומי

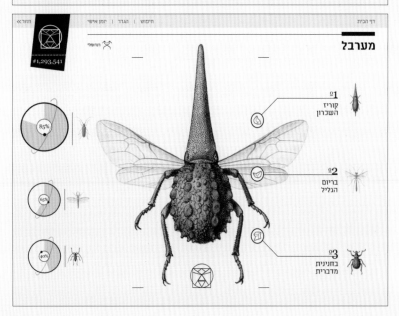

85%

65%

40%

1
קוריז
השכרון

2
בריום
הגליל

3
בחנינית
מדברית

מגדיר חרקים

#1,293,541

השוואה · מערבי · מסדר · תרגומי

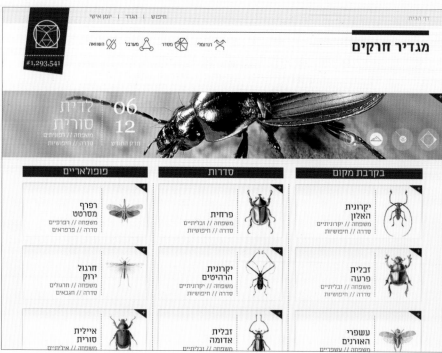

06
12 לדית סורית
מדריך החודש
משפחה // רמוניתים
סדרה // חיפושיות

פופולאריים

רפרף מסרטט
משפחה // רפריפים
סדרה // רפרפאים

חרגול ירוק
משפחה // חרגולים
סדרה // חגבאים

איילית סורית
משפחה // איליתיים

סדרות

פרחית
משפחה // זבליתים
סדרה // חיפושיות

יקרונית הרריטים
משפחה // יקרוניתיים
סדרה // חיפושיות

זבלית אדומה
משפחה // זבליתים

בקרבת מקום

יקרונית האלון
משפחה // יקרוניתיים
סדרה // חיפושיות

זבלית פרעה
משפחה // זבליתים
סדרה // חיפושיות

עשפרי האורנים
משפחה // עשפריים

#1,293,541

צילומים · סטטיסטיקה

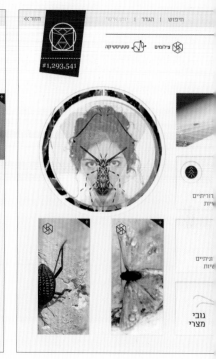

רוריתיים
שיות

ונתיים
שיות

גובי
מצרי

גל סיני

#1,293,541

צילומים · סטטיסטיקה

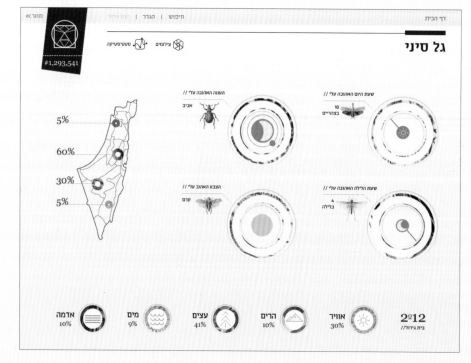

5%
60%
30%
5%

העונה האהובה עלי //
אביב

שעת היום האהובה עלי //
10 בצהריים

הצבע האהוב עלי //
קרם

שעת הלילה האהובה עלי //
4 בלילה

אדמה
10%

מים
9%

עצים
41%

הרים
10%

אוויר
30%

2º12
בית גידול //

#1,293,541

צילומים · סטטיסטיקה

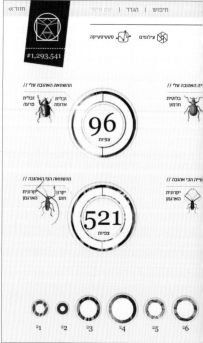

השוואה האהובה עלי //
זבלית פרעה
אדומה

96
צפיות

השוואה הכי אהובה //
יקרונית
חום

521
צפיות

ייה האהובה עלי //
בלוטית
חומה

עייה הכי אהובה //
יקרונית
הארגמן

№1 №2 №3 №4 №5 №6

גל סיני

זבלית אדומה

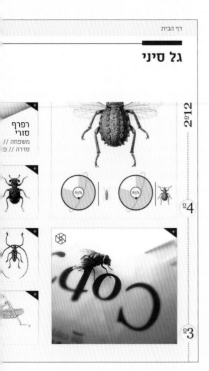

2º12

רפרף
סורי
משפחה //
סדרה // פ

º4

º3

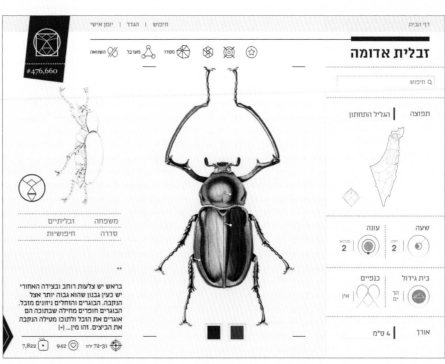

#476,660

השוואה | מעורב' | מוסדר

חיפוש

| תפוצה | הגליל התחתון |

| שעה | עונה |
| 2 | 2 |

| בית גידול | כנפיים |
| הר ים | אין |

| אורך | 4 ס"מ |

משפחה   זבליתיים
סדרה   חיפושיות

**

בראש יש צלעות רוחב ובצידה האחורי
יש כעין גבנון שהוא גבוה יותר אצל
הנקבה. הבוגרים והזחלים ניזונים מזבל.
הבוגרים חופרים מחילה שבתוכה הם
אוגרים את הזבל ולתוכו מטילה הנקבה
את הביצים. זהו מין... [+]

7,822   942 ♡   72-31

גל סיני

מסדר חרקים

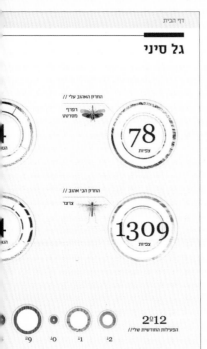

החרק האהוב עלי //

רפרף
מסרטט

78
צפיות

החרק הכי אהוב //

צרצר

1309
צפיות

2º12
הפעילות החודשית שלי//

º9   º0   º1   º2

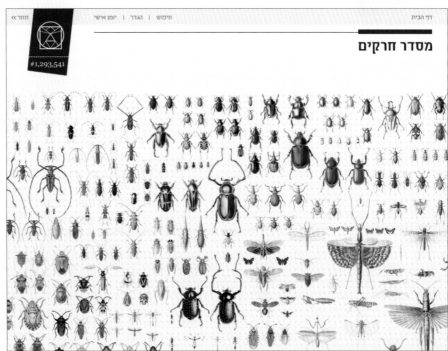

#1,293,541

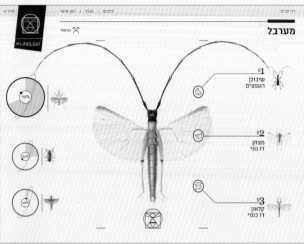

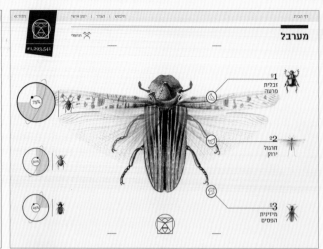

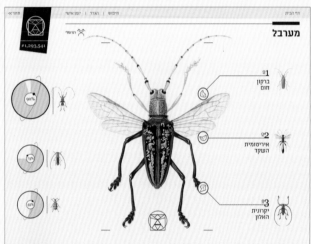

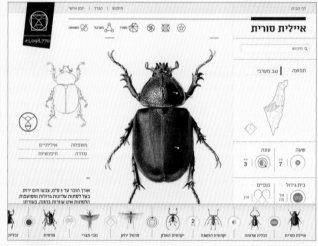

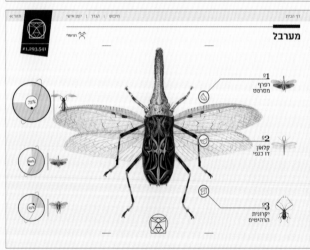

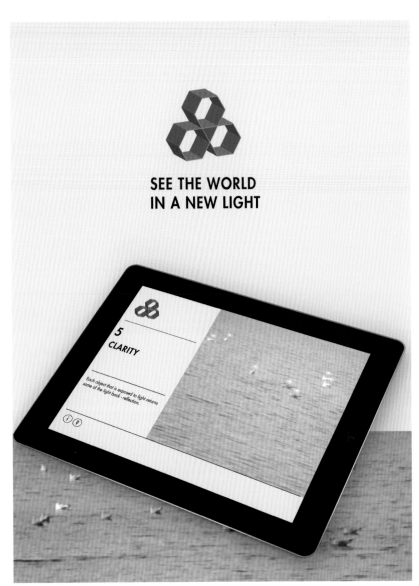

See the World in a New Light

This is a science app that demonstrates the effect of light on our planet. It's a way of looking at the everyday and ordinary with a new perspective—science is everywhere. The app is placed in public spaces such as Hayarkon Park in Tel Aviv, Israel, in order to teach people the different effects of light. Six major points throughout the park were chosen to place the app. In each area, the user can run the application, photograph the area and get more information about the light phenomenon that occurs.

 Yael Cohen

 Israel

 www.yaelco.com

1-6

SEE THE WORLD IN A NEW LIGHT

It's a way of looking at the everyday and ordinary with a new perspective - science is everywhere.

Photon · Refraction · Light & Water · Dispersion · Clarity · Diffraction

ⓘ ⑦

2

REFRACTION & BREAKAGE

The bending of the light rays when passing through a surface between one transparent material to another, breakage of light changes its direction.

Refraction · Break

ⓘ ⑦

BIBLIOGRAPHY -

SEE THE WORLD IN A NEW LIGHT

Light Project // photograph - Yarkon Park, Tel Aviv, Israel // by Yael Cohen

Light Science and Magic, Fourth Edition: An Introduction to Photographic Lighting // by Fil Hunter, Paul Fuqua and Steven Biver // 2004

QED: The Strange Theory of Light and Matter (Princeton Science Library) // by Richard P. Feynman and A. Zee // 2006

The Bible, the Qur'an and Science: The Holy Scriptures Examined in the Light of Modern Knowledge, translated from the French // by Maurice Bucaille and Alastair D. Pannell // 1989

Handbook of Photovoltaic Science and Engineering // by Antonio Luque and Steven Hegedus // 1998

Seeing the Light: Optics in Nature, Photography, and Holography // by David R. Falk // 1986

The Story of Light: Path to Enlightenment // by S. Roger Joyeux // 1981

The Illuminating World of Light with Max Axiom, Super Scientist (Graphic Science) (Graphic Library: Graphic Science) // by Emily Sohn // 2008

Light and Color // by Clarence Rainwater // 2011

Geometry and Light: The Science of Invisibility (Dover Books on Physics) // by Ulf Leonhardt, Thomas Philbin and Physics // 2010

Uncommon Knowledge: New Science of Gravity, Light, the Origin of Life, and the Mind of Man // by Al McDowell // 2010

ⓘ ⑦

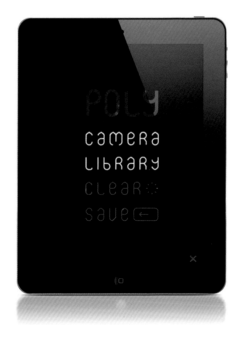

Poly™

Poly is a creative application for iPad. This project was inspired by the triangulation invented by the mathematician Boris Delaunay in 1934. While the process behind is complicated, the result reduces an image to its essentials, creating the illusions of triangles, prisms and pyramids. Poly will let users draw with points and turn pictures into geometric array of colors.

 Jean-Christophe NAOUR

 Innoiz Interactive

 South Korea

 www.jcnaour.com

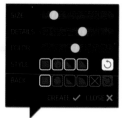

Pixl™

Pixl is a creative tool for iPhone and iPad that helps people to rediscover their pictures. They can play with several settings including adjusting the size of the pixels, the color and the contrast or select patterns to use. This is a new interactive experience to explore pixels and colors behind photography and to create countless combinations of fantastic imagery with a simple touch.

Jean-Christophe NAOUR

Innoiz Inc.

South Korea

www.jcnaour.com

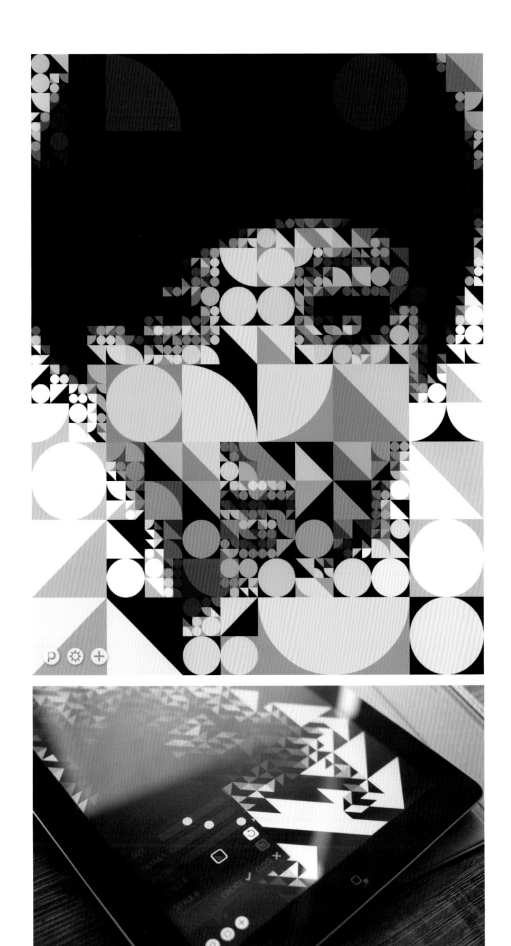

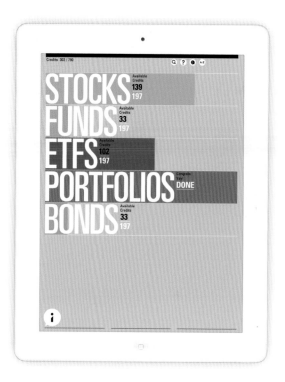

Morningstar Investing Classroom

Morningstar Investing Classroom is an iPad application helping individual investors to learn about funds, stocks, bonds, etc. It uses various typographic treatments (mainly contrast), and animations to display the layers of contents. This allows for intuitive navigation in using the app.

 Pouya Ahmadi

 Victor Savolainen

 Morningstar Inc.

 USA

 www.pouyaahmadi.com

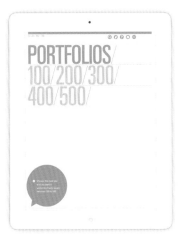

Deckadance

Deckadance is an app that can turn your iPad or iPhone into a DJ virtual mixing system. Initially it was just an iPad app, which made sense since the iPad has a display big enough for the application. Later on the designers reworked the UI and designed an iPhone version to fulfill the client's new requirement. They used some popular musical devices as reference, and tried to make the user experience as exciting and realistic as possible after they realized that a tactile feeling would not reflect in the former version.

 Eugene Cheporov

 Eugene Cheporov

 Artua LLC

 Image-Line

 USA

www.artua.com

Infinity Restaurant Menu App

In this UI, circular menus were used in a different way, creating a fresh feeling and offering an effective way to manage space. The client wanted a royal atmosphere, while the designer a modern one. The designer finally settled the dissent with a sumptuous background and lighting, in combination of modern buttons and sleek fonts.

 Barjinder Singh

 Rahul Panwar

 India

 http://www.mrsingh.pro

Domotic System

"Domo" means home in Latin, while "-otic" stands for robotic, so the word domotic refers to "home automation". This is a prototype GUI, designed for a system which integrates the control of audio, video, lighting, blinds, air conditioners, video surveillance and appliances in a single remote control manageable from a single tablet. The simple and relatively large icons as well as an overview of the general situation, at any time, are the key points of the design. The GUI has been designed to be operated in "landscape mode" using two hands, as if it were a joystick—the left hand browses through options, while the right hand interacts with the section.

Simone Giannangeli

Italy

www.behance.net/sgiannangeli

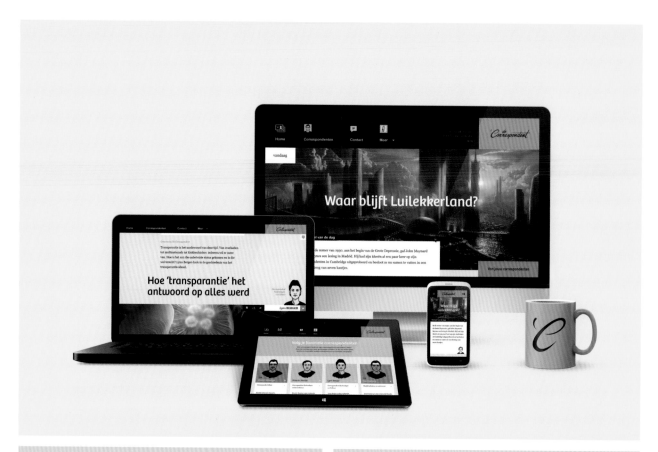

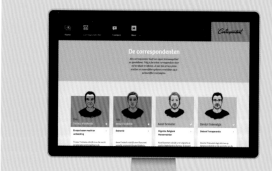

De Correspondent

De Correspondent is an on-line journalism platform in Dutch with a fully responsive design. When users login, they receive a daily newsfeed. Users can scroll down easily to read previous daily issues and follow their favorite correspondents via a handy sidebar. Each correspondent has a homepage with stories he or she published. Next to the website the designer built their own editor called Respondens, a new kind of CMS allowing correspondents to truly function as conversation leaders.

Harald Dunnink, Martijn van Dam, Cléa Dieudonné

Momkai

De Correspondent

The Netherlands

www.decorrespondent.nl

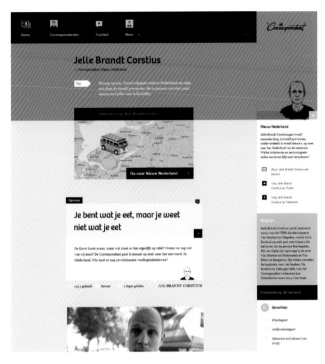

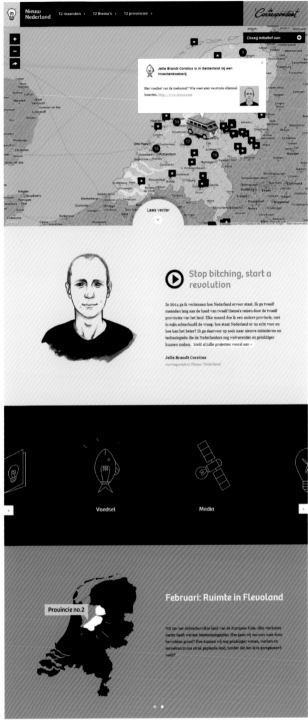

New Netherlands

New Netherlands is an innovative experience on De Correspondent. Jelle Brandt Corstius explores The Netherlands while asking: "how can things be improved?" Each of the twelve provinces is assigned a different theme and the author visits a new region monthly. Members add their ideas via a special site, putting their initiatives on the map.

Harald Dunnink, Cléa Dieudonné

Momkai

De Correspondent

The Netherlands

https://decorrespondent.nl/nieuw-nederland

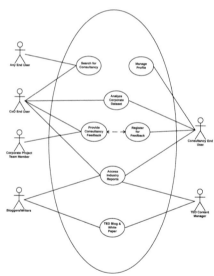

TiC: UX/UI Design Work

TiC (Transparency in Consulting) is a powerful analytic tool to help analyze people's recent consulting projects. It helps users to do things like benchmark their service and discover how to get more value from consulting. TiC provides insight that doesn't exist in the market today. It provides information like ratings, feedback, consulting directory, analysis/bench marking of consulting services received (for CxO) and analysis of customer opinions about the consultant.

 Naresh Kumar

Transparency in Consulting

 India

 uikreative.com

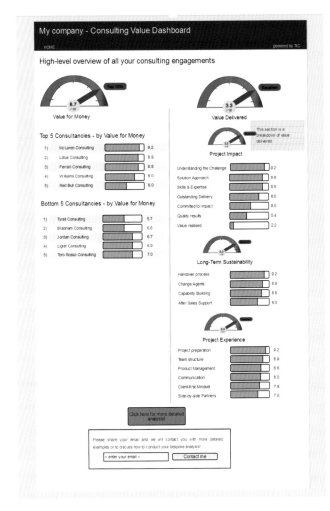

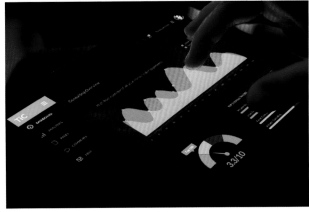

Nuvola Base

Nuvola Base is a website powered by OrientDB. Users can utilize, share and exchange databases online. Nuvola means cloud in Italian and a sun is the current logo of OrientDB. So the designer designed a sun behind a cloud as the logo of this new service.

The designer used very simple graphics, with straightforward icons for easy comprehension. The basic idea is that despite the considerable technological expertise behind Nuvola Base, sharing information is a first priority.

 Simone Giannangeli

 Italy

 www.behance.net/sgiannangeli

Jack's Pot

Jack's Pot is an educational web experience focused on important financial principals for young children. The project was designed summarizing the learning experience and adapting an interesting storyline which children can relate to. The designers intended to seamlessly engage children in a series of challenges where they need to use medium-term planning and resource management to solve in-game problems. The narrative was based on athletic competitions. The user could choose a contest by selecting icons with vivid pictures on them.

 Carine Teyrouz

 Lebanon (project worked in Barcelona)

 www.behance.net/gallery/JacksPot-Responsive-Webdesign/10734629

Plock World

Plock World is a popular game on Facebook that features colorful crystalline blocks and child-friendly items. It's an exciting and appealing game for both children and adults. What the players need to do is break the blocks by matching two or more of the same color, playing through different levels and amazing adventures. The players can share the scores and challenge their friends.

 Valeria Matos

 Metrogames

 Argentina

 https://www.behance.net/valeriamatos

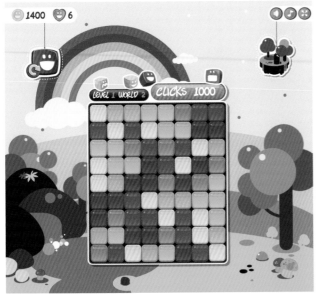

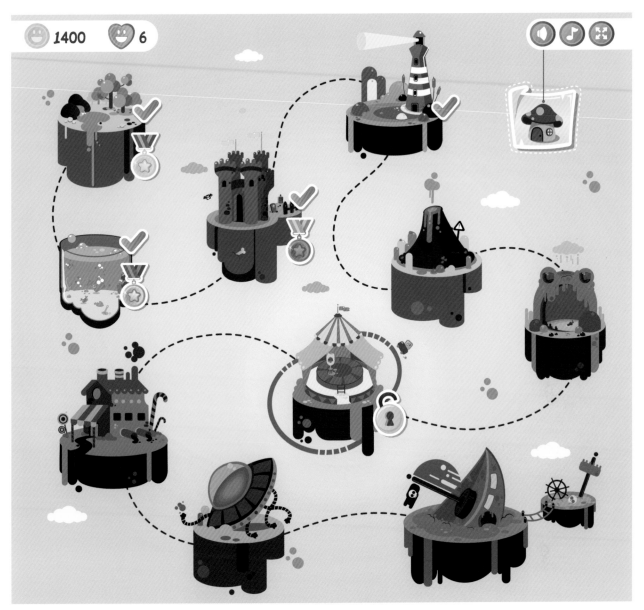

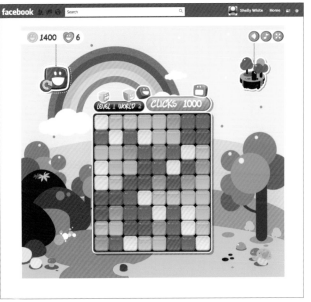

Stamp Frenzy

Stamp Frenzy is a social game on Facebook for virtual stamp collectors. The game provides a large number of different sets and series. Users can collect stamps and display their collections in an on-line exhibition hall. The creation of the game's wireframe, the complete new GUI approach and the design makeover are about preserving the stockbook feeling to the game. Since it is a classic game transposed into the virtual world, the interface had to preserve that atmosphere. To that end, the designer used fabric and wood-like textures and different objects to set up a real and familiar context.

Ovidiu Bejan; Erik Erdokozi

Sorin Bechira

eRepublik Labs

Romania

http://wearex3.com/

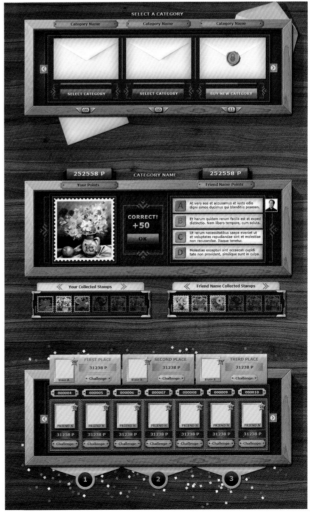

Planning for issues that may arise from the beginning, making use of some of the resources listed below and consulting users who are drawn from a wide ranging pool of potential customers (but above all representative user group) are all meaningful goals when designing GUIs.

It is sensible to test your GUI on as many different browsers, devices and connections as possible.

It will probably be useful to make a distinction between your core users (those for whom the collection has been intended and is primarily targeted) and your extended users (those who may also derive some benefit from it).

Where there are contradictory suggestions or resource limitations, it is likely that you will favor the needs and suggestions of your core users over your extended user base. However, in some cases you might decide that you need to provide more than one GUI for your project.

All too often, those planning digital projects are concentrated more on their data collection and characteristics than on their users and the users' needs. But this always leads to a scramble to find certain users and convince them that they can benefit from the resource.

Large widgets, like windows, usually provide a frame or container for the main presentation content (web pages, email message, drawings etc.). Smaller ones usually act as a user-input tool.

If you decide to serve a number of different audiences, you may have to offer completely different GUIs to each group.

The visual widgets of a well-designed interface are selected to support the actions necessary to achieve the goals of the user.

Designing the visual composition and temporal behavior of GUI is an important step in enhancing the efficiency and ease of use for the underlying logical design of a stored program, a design discipline known as usability.

PUSHABLE BEZEL FOR NAVIGATION

PUSHERS FOR
BUILT-IN FUNCTIONS

CROWN FOR
BUILT-IN FUNCTIONS
AND SETUP

PUSHERS FOR
BUILT-IN FUNCTIONS

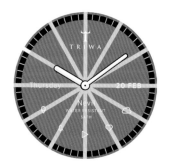

Smartwatch

In this design, the designer achieved a wide range of goals including a wrist watch
on which videos and pop-up notifications are shown on the same surface. The
smartwatch can be a combination of tradition and technology.

 Gábor Balogh

 Hungary

 www.behance.net/baloghgabor

POST. US Weather Forecaster

Inspired by notes pinned on refrigerators and doors as a reminder and family commutation tool, the designer came up with an idea to make a weather forecaster which could help families to share more and communicate more in today's busy life. For family, weather would be a daily topic to talk about with each other. This conceptual user experience design uses a transparent touch screen material, with multiple functions to improve the "post-it" on our refrigerators in a modern way and enrich our experience of communication.

 Junyao Feng

 USA

 www.jy-feng.com

FOUR MODES. Weather Mode

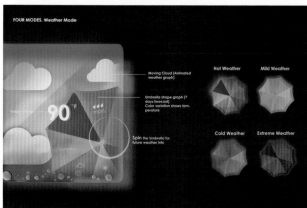

Moving Cloud (Animated weather graph)

Umbrella shape graph (7 days forecast)
Color variation shows temperature

Spin the Umbrella for future weather info

Hot Weather   Mild Weather

Cold Weather   Extreme Weather

FOUR MODES. Message Mode

FOUR MODES. Message Mode

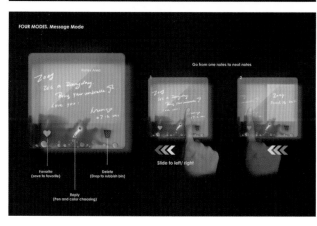

Notes Area

Go from one notes to next notes

Slide to left/ right

Favorite
(save to favorite)

Delete
(Drop to rubbish bin)

Reply
(Pen and color choosing)

FOUR MODES. Message Mode

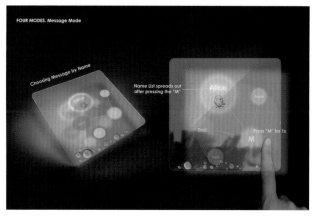

Choosing Message by Name

Name List spreads out after pressing the "M"

Alice

Press "M" for 1s

FOUR MODES. Photo Mode

Rainy Day

Photos and Videos show with the info. of weather

Sunny Day   Snow Day

FOUR MODES. Game Mode

Game mode offer multiple games to play with when you are in the kitchen.
For example, decorate the pictures.

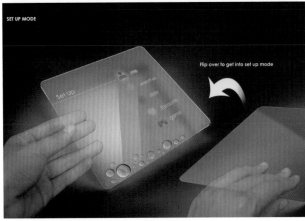

SET UP MODE

Set Up

Flip over to get into set up mode

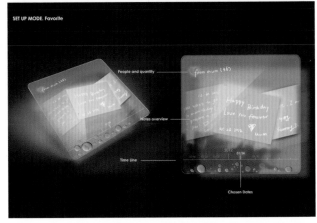

SET UP MODE. Favorite

People and quantity

Notes overview

Time Line

Chosen Dates

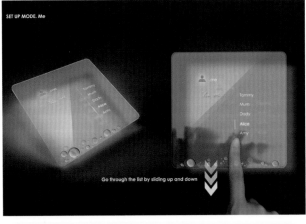

SET UP MODE. Me

Tommy
Mum
Dady
Alice
Amy

Go through the list by sliding up and down

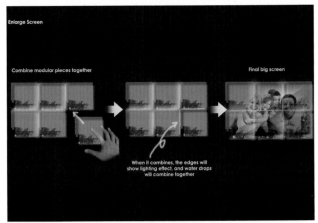

Enlarge Screen

Combine modular pieces together   Final big screen

When it combines, the edges will
show lighting effect, and water drops
will combine together

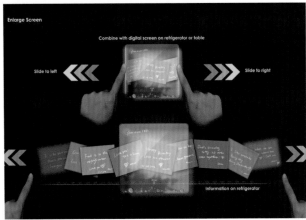

Enlarge Screen

Combine with digital screen on refrigerator or table

Slide to left   Slide to right

Information on refrigerator

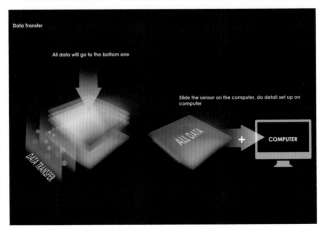

Data Transfer

All data will go to the bottom one

Slide the sensor on the computer, do detail set up on
computer

DATA TRANSFER   ALL DATA   +   COMPUTER

FOUR MODES

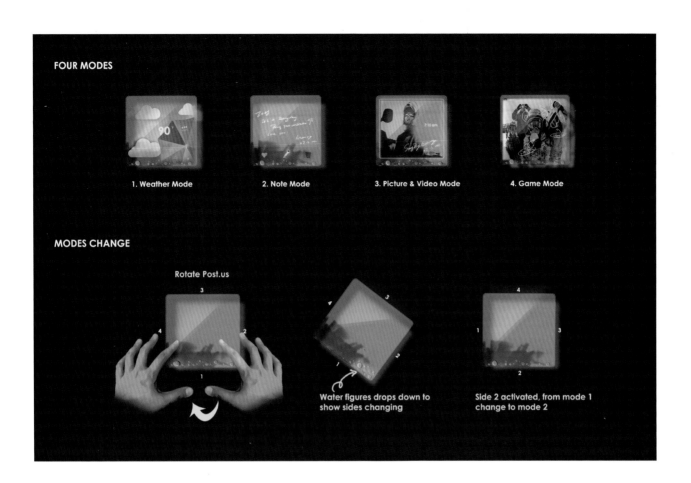

1. Weather Mode
2. Note Mode
3. Picture & Video Mode
4. Game Mode

MODES CHANGE

Rotate Post.us

Water figures drops down to
show sides changing

Side 2 activated, from mode 1
change to mode 2

DIFFERENT CONCEPT

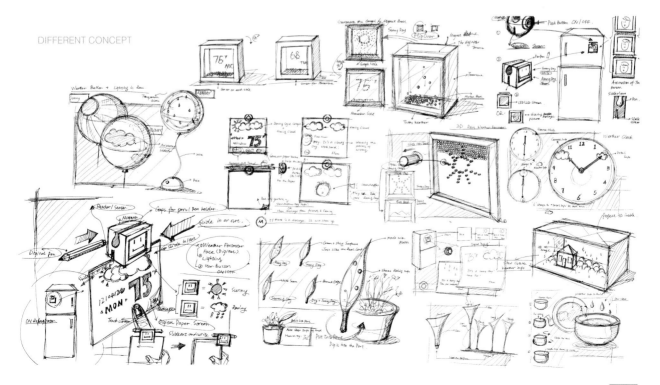

Kinect Graffiti™

Kinect Graffiti™ is a digital graffiti tool using "Microsoft Kinect" camera. The idea behind this project is to use the Kinect to track the motion behind graffiti, and to visualize the body and drawings through different angles in real time. The Designer used the 3D data from camera and reproduced digitally the trails appearing on a long exposure photography. This explains its aesthetic reference from that luminous form of graffiti: light painting.

 Jean-Christophe NAOUR

 Innoiz Inc.

 South Korea

 www.jcnaour.com

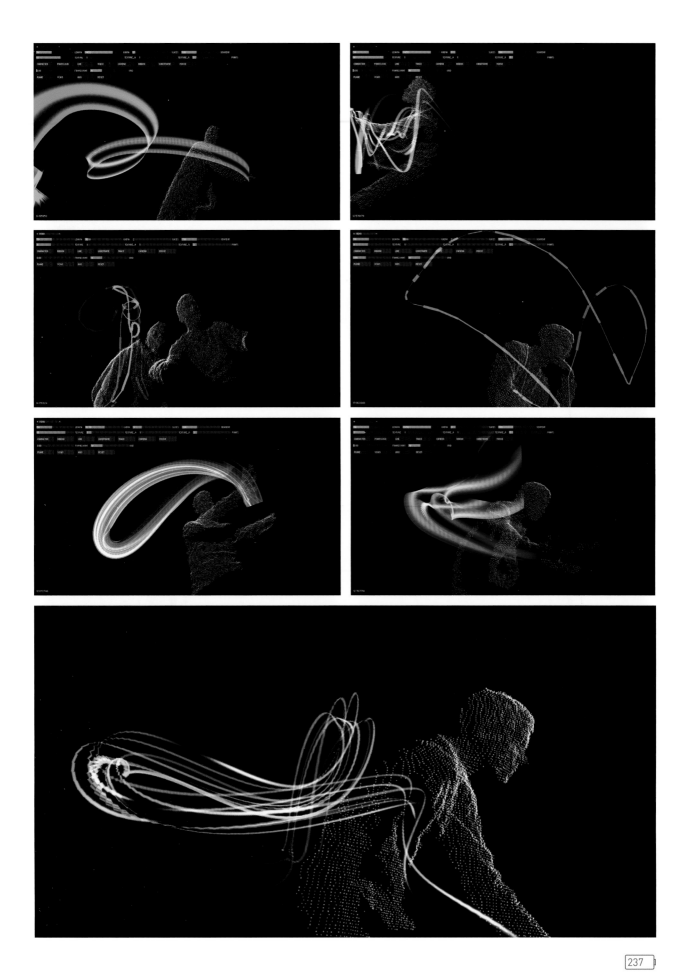

Flix Movie Interface

The Flix interface project was designed as a forward-thinking touchscreen interface to view and manage the transfer of digital movies to theatres all around the world.

The concept is centered around a large touchscreen, making the interface both beautiful and informative and at the same time easy to interact with. Data can be displayed visually as infographics, by geography, and in clear patterns that allow users to easily access and view data in a delightfully intuitive way. The project also explored branding for Flix, considering different platforms and an extended ecosystem of technological capabilities.

 Thomas Moeller

 United Kingdom

 www.thomasmoeller.com

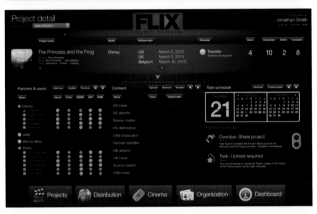

UI Interactive Elements

Buttons
1. CONTROLS AND INTERACTIVE ELEMENTS

Project thumbnails
2. TITLE GRAPHICS AND ASSETS

Calendar
3. CALENDAR UI AND COMPONENTS

Icons
4. ICONOGRAPHY AND GRAPHICAL LANGUAGE

TV가이드 *GUIDE*   실시간TV *LIVETV*   동영상 *VOD*   스포츠 *SPORTS*   키즈팡 *KIDS*   앱스 *APPS*   인터넷 *INTERNET*   설정 *SET*

PM 10:30

DAUM TV+

The DAUM TV+ GUI was designed by DOUBLEDOT in a way that the identity of the menu icon of each content category is utilized, and visibility is increased so that the contents which the user is looking for can be found and explored more easily. With the simple, intuitive set top box or remote control, it can be optimized for usability. Also, the creators designed the icons representing the main features and functions, which were done on the basis of the GUI of DAUM TV+, to move freely and dynamically inside the TV box. They want to express the joyful, pleasant and unique image of DAUM TV+, and design it so that the entire DAUM TV+ GUI and BI can be harmonized in a consistent flow at the same time.

 Hyoung Shin Park/ Hyoung Suk Kim/ Minjung Gong/ Miyoung Park/ Sunhwa Lee

 Hyoung Shin Park

 DOUBLEDOT

DAUM

Korea

 www.doubledot.co.kr

Daum TV+ GUI design / install

INSTALL
설치화면

—

Daum TV+ GUI design / vod

VOD SELECTING MODE
VOD 선택 모드

—

Daum TV+ GUI design / web

INTERNET BROWSING . CONTEXT MENU
인터넷 브라우징

—

Daum TV+ GUI design / setting

SETTING
환경설정

—

Daum TV+ GUI design / flicking main

2ND DEPTH / MAIN PAGES : 6-FACE ROTATION
카테고리별 상위 메인화면

—

Daum TV+ GUI design / guide

ICON
아이콘

FLICK

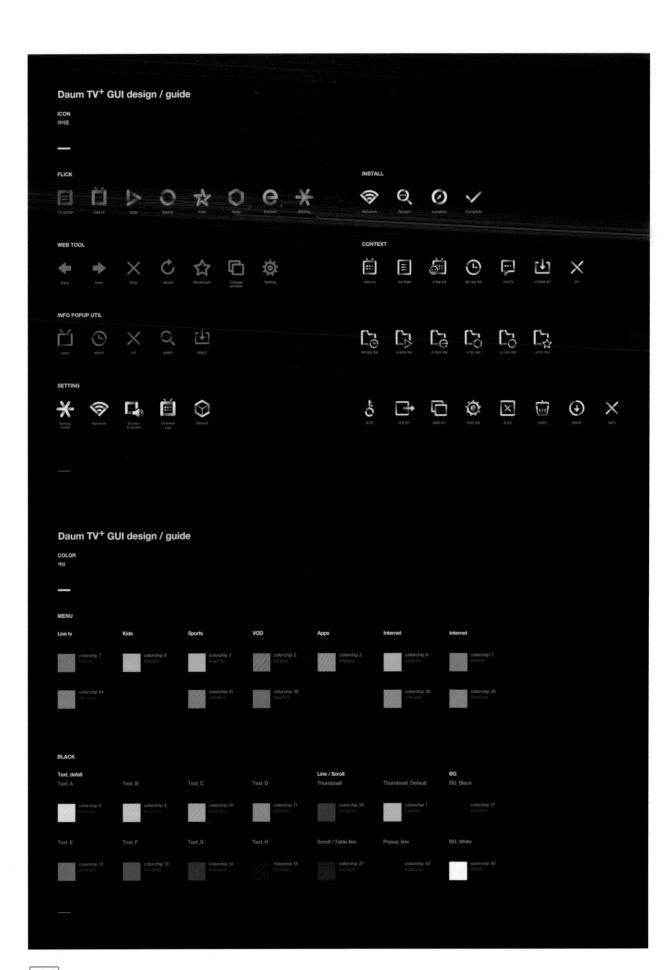

TV guide　Live tv　VOD　Sports　Kids　Apps　Internet　Setting

INSTALL

Network　Screen　Location　Complete

WEB TOOL

Back　Next　Stop　reload　Bookmark　Change window　Setting

CONTEXT

INFO POPUP UTIL

SETTING

Setting home　Network　Screen & sound　Channel List　Device

Daum TV+ GUI design / guide

COLOR
색상

MENU

Live tv	Kids	Sports	VOD	Apps	Internet	Internet
colorchip 7 #5f51ff	colorchip 5 #tfb245	colorchip 3 #aef732	colorchip 2 #ff3451	colorchip 2 #ff695a	colorchip 6 #00e1fm	colorchip 7 #5f91ff
colorchip 34		colorchip 41 #7b9673	colorchip 35 #9az7575		colorchip 36 #7ba0af	colorchip 34 #8b291b8

BLACK

Text_defalt

Text_A	Text_B	Text_C	Text_D	Line / Scroll Thumbnail	Thumbnail_Default	BG BG_Black
colorchip 8 #efefefe5	colorchip 9 #cacscfc	colorchip 10 #b2b2b2	colorchip 11 #999999	colorchip 26 #535353	colorchip 1 #bf0fbf	colorchip 17 #000000

Text_E	Text_F	Text_G	Text_H	Scroll / Table line	Popup_line	BG_White
colorchip 12 #8f6b90	colorchip 13 #6b5b66	colorchip 14 #d4d4d4	colorchip 15 #333333	colorchip 27 #454640	colorchip 42 #2a2a2a	colorchip 40 #ffffff

---

242

Daum TV⁺ BI design / tv logo image

RETRO TV + NEW SMART = DAUM TV
아날로그 TV에도 셋탑연결만으로 스마트TV가 될 수 있다는 의미의 로고.

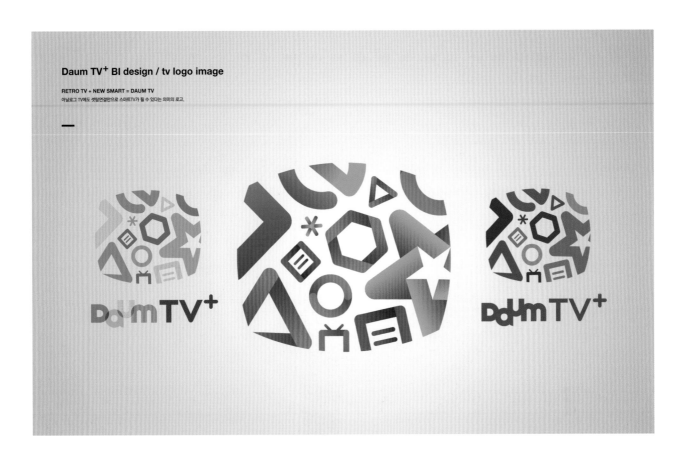

Daum TV⁺ GUI design / guide

LAYOUT
레이아웃

전체메뉴

A Contents
주요 컨텐츠

B Information Area
관련정보노출

A Title Area
해당 카테고리 열

B Location Area
전체메뉴 중 현재 위치 노출

C Contents
주요 컨텐츠

LG UPLUS TV GUI

This design is a reinterpretation of the brand identity of LG Uplus. Switching to the secretary mode, movies and TV programs can be searched and recommended based on users' preference. Different view modes are provided and within users' choices. It contains a real-time visual searching system, where popular words, persons and content are exposed as images and can be targeted with key operations. The design complies with the guideline of Google TV and the business directions of LG Uplus service.

 Hyoung Shin Park/ Sanwon Yu/ Eunhee Jo/ Donghee Roh/ Daesung Huh/ Seyoon Kim/ Minjung Gong/ Miyoung Park

LG UPLUS

Korea

 www.doubledot.co.kr

LG U⁺ TV G GUI design / Search

EXPLORING SEARCH MODE
실시간 인기 아이템도

LG U⁺ TV G GUI design / VOD detail popup #2

CONTENTS DETAIL VIEW
VOD 콘텐츠 상세보기

LG U⁺ TV G GUI design / VOD detail popup #1

CONTENTS DETAIL VIEW
사진 콘텐츠 나열보기

LG U⁺ TV G GUI design / VOD play controller #2

IMAGE BROWSING MODE
영상 재생하기

LG U⁺ TV G GUI design / "U" mode

PERSONALIZED CONTENT RECOMMENDATION
개인 특화 컨텐츠 추천기능

Daum TV⁺ BI design

IDEA
아이디어

SKETCH
스케치

FINAL DESIGN
최종 디자인

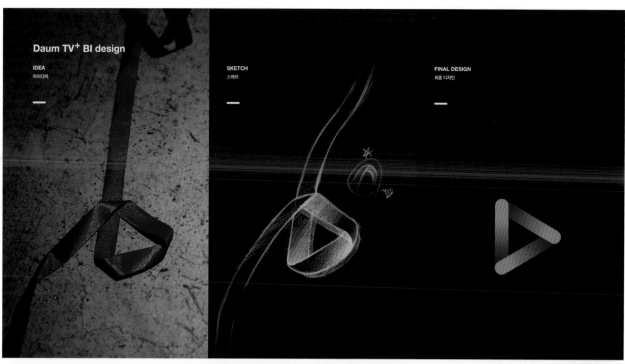

Daum TV⁺ BI design

REAL-OBJECT
일반형태 이미지

SIMPLIFYING DRAWING
단순화 드로잉

CONCEPT SKETCH
컨셉 스케치

FINAL DESIGN
최종 디자인

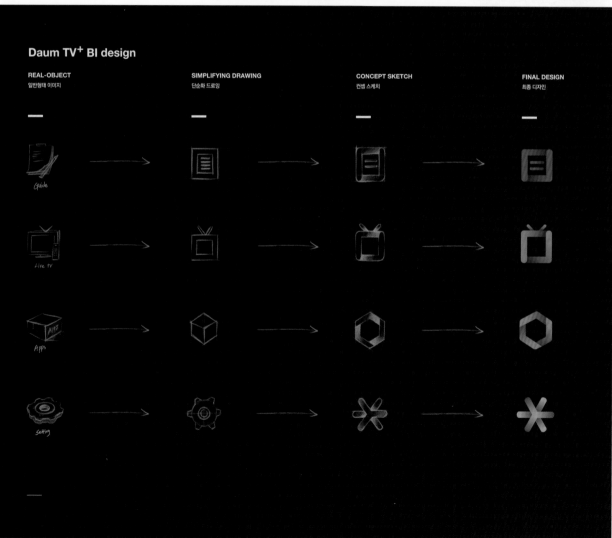

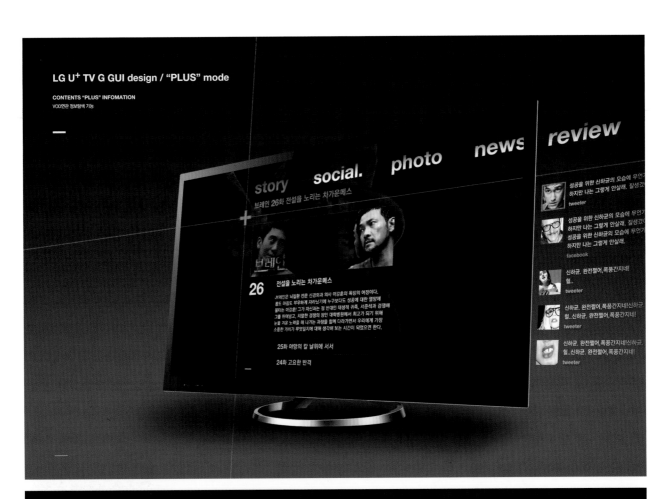

LG U⁺ TV G GUI design / "PLUS" mode

CONTENTS "PLUS" INFOMATION
VOD연관 정보탐색 기능

LG U⁺ TV G GUI design / Final design

FINAL DESIGN
최종디자인

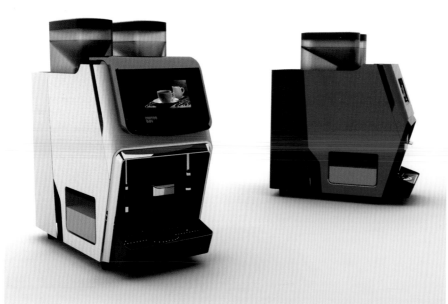

Celesta Touch

This design was inspired by the concept of minimalism and simplicity. It is simple and intuitive not because of the absence of clutter, but because of the the clarity and cohesiveness it provides to users. The device would "stay out of the way" while someone was using the touch interface, and their interaction with the device would seem natural. The design achieved a balance in type, color and shapes.

 Sarath S Nair

 Coffee Day Design

 India

 https://www.behance.net/sarathsnair

A latte is sometimes served in a bowl; in Europe, particularly **Scandinavia**, this is referred to as a **cafe au lait.**

Throughout the world, there are more than 6 billion consumers of **milk** and **milk products**.

CELESTA TOUCH COFFEE MACHINE ICONS

CAPPUCCINO   ESPRESSO   LATTE   TEA   MILK   HOT WATER

CANCEL   INBOX   FUN ZONE   MY ACCOUNT   BANGALORE 24°C   STEAM

CANCELLING   BLEND A

GUI for Skoda Citigo Electric Cars

The goal of this project was to create a touchscreen GUI for the Skoda Citigo electric car which could quickly and clearly convey the driver's information to the car. For ergonomic and safety reasons, the instrumental panel and media center were placed under the windshield in the middle of dashboard.

The whole concept put a lot of emphasis on drivers' safety. The user will only see the most important information on the screen. The interactive items are large and will stay in their settled positions. The key function of volume in the media center can be controlled by gesture without distracting the driver.

 MgA. Ondrej Velebny

 MgA. Ondrej Velebny,
Škoda Auto a.s.

 Czech Republic

 www.gdschameleon.cz

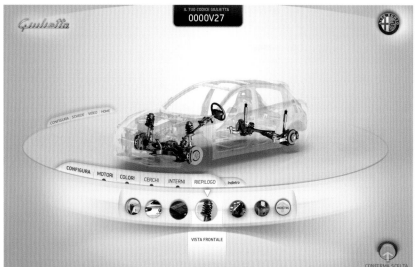

Interactive Kiosk

This is a user interface for 220 interactive items found all around Italy positioned in the Alfa Romeo dealerships. The interface is controlled by a knob through Arduino. Users are able to browse and select any of the contents by rotating and pressing the knob. The car configuration area of the system allows users to create their own car while the other discovery areas provide a platform for users to discover all the new features from the car by video and information cards.

 Gianpaolo Tucci & Andrea Piccolo

 Alfa Romeo

 Italy

 www.gianpaolotucci.com

Comfort

Il posto del guidatore è stato studiato per accogliere, con una posizione ergonomicamente corretta, persone alte fino a 192 cm cioè il 99% della popolazione. Si possono accogliere contemporaneamente al posto di guida persone di 185 cm e posteriormente passeggeri alti fino a 180 cm.

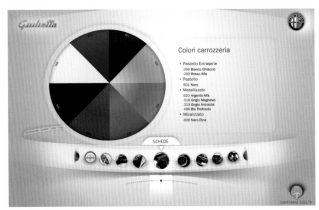

Colori carrozzeria

- Pastello Extraserie
  296 Bianco Ghiaccio
  289 Rosso Alfa
- Pastello
  601 Nero
- Metallizzato
  620 Argento Alfa
  318 Grigio Magnesio
  319 Grigio Antracite
  486 Blu Profondo
- Micalizzato
  806 Nero Etna

Tecnologia

- Impianto HI-FI BOSE che raggiunge livelli di acustica eccellente, anche grazie ai 10 altoparlanti previsti e all'amplificatore 8800.
- Blue&Me, che prevede la connessione telefono Bluetooth, comandi vocali, lettura vocale SMS, porta USB e MP3 Media Player;
- Radionavigatore a mappa a scomparsa, con funzionalità audio (Radio, CD e SD), navigazione a mappe, informazioni vettura (services e Trip Computer), informazioni DNA;
- Dispositivo Alfa D.N.A
- Fari Bi-xenon con funzione AFS

Interni

Giulietta

INDEX

ACKNOWLEDGEMENTS

We would like to thank all the designers and contributers who have been involved in the production of this book. Their contribution is indispensable in the compilation of this book. We would also like to express our gratitude to all the producers for their invaluable opinions and assistance throughout this project. And to the many others whose names are not credited but have made specific input in this book, we thank you for your continuous support.

FUTURE COOPERATIONS: If you wish to participate in SendPoints' future projects and publications, please send your website or portfolio to editor01@sendpoints.cn